Skinny Malinky Long Legs:

Tales from La Scala Cinema, Clydebank

ROGER CLIFFORD

ISBN: 978-1-7396113-0-9
Edited and Typeset in the UK by Beech Editorial
Services

DEDICATION

A special thank you to the following people who have helped me pursue my aim of writing and producing this book: Roger Clifford (Jnr), Colette Duggan (Beech Editorial Services), Margaret Finnie and Mary Frances McGlynn (Arts & Heritage -Dumbarton Library)

OTHER TITLES
I Just Went Out for Bread and Milk

ACKNOWLEDGEMENTS

Many people have generously granted their permission to use their photos, poems, drawings and paintings in this book. However if there are any omissions, these will be corrected in future editions.

DISCLAIMER

While I have made every effort to be as accurate as possible with the information relating to dates, times, photos, etc. in this book, it is possible that some errors remain. These are not meant to be misleading, and all endeavours have been made to make the book as accurate as possible.

The language in this book reflects the usage of the times and is not intended to cause any offence.

Roger Clifford

List of Illustrations

Photograph permissions

Photographs	Courtesy of:
1, 4–8, 16, 23, 20, 25, 31	Arts & Heritage Dumbarton Library
2	Hugh Gillan
3	Martin Kennedy
9–12	Moving Image Archive (Scotland)
13	Eldorado
14	James Kissack
15	Boyd McNicol
17–20	Christine Pert
21	Len Smyth
22	Permission sought - St Andrew's University Archive – Valentine Collection
24	Brian Prince
26	Danny Smith
27	Billy Bellingham (Jnr)
28	Andrew McGhie
29, 30	Clydebank Press
32	Gary McLaren
33	David Skewis (Jnr)
34, 36, 37	Gordon McGowan
35	John Albiston
38	Roger Clifford
39	Tam McColl

Contents

Skinny Malinky Long Legs,
Big banana feet.
Went to the pictures,
But couldnae find a seat.
When the pictures started,
Skinny Malinky farted!
Skinny Malinky Long Legs,
Big banana feet.

Timeline

13–15 March 1941 Clydebank Blitz

31 July 1969 La Scala Bingo opened

1984 La Scala Crucible Club opened

1930s Clydebank Wedderlea Dance Hall was built

14 Feb 1938 – Cinema opened

31 August 1959 – La Scala was taken over by Associated British Cinemas

12 April 1964 – Closed on for conversion into a bingo hall and a 776-seat cinema

31 July 1969 –reopened

19 Feb 1983 – Cinema was closed for good

2006 – Bingo Hall was closed

2013 – Public auction of the site

What was happening in 1938?

La Scala was built in Clydebank.

The monarch on the throne was George VI.

Joseph Kennedy (father of President John F Kennedy) was named as America's Ambassador to the United Kingdom.

The famous Beano comic by D.C. Thompson goes on sale for the first time, featuring characters like Lord Snooty.

The *Queen Elizabeth* is launched in Clydebank in Sept 1938. It was constructed at the John Brown shipyard. At the time it was the largest ship in the world.

Angus Mackenzie publishes *The Foundations of Scotland*, the first of a six-volume history.

East Fife (Football Team) wins the Scottish Cup. Oh, yes they did!

J Arthur Rank purchases Odeon Cinemas.

Paul Daniels Magician was born.

London's Children's Zoo opened.

Kellogg's Corn Flakes - Although the brand was born in

rural Midwest America, the first UK factory opened in Manchester in 1938.

Orson Wells's radio adaption of *War of the Worlds*. It was reported that it caused panic and fear due to actors' realistic voice work and the background sounds, however, the panic was possibly made up by newspapers themselves.

Cost of living when La Scala opened in 1938

Loaf of bread - around two pence

Pint of milk - around the same, two pence

Average cost of house rent - between five to ten shillings a week

A terraced house - between £600 and £750

A gallon of fuel - ten pence

Average wage - about £165 per year

The average price of a new car - around £170

£100 in 1938 was equivalent in today's prices (2022) to approximately £7,000

The very first showing at the cinema on the 14 February 1938 was *Maytime* staring the popular musical duo of Jeanette MacDonald and Nelson Eddie.

A Trip down Memory Lane

The following is a collection of my own experiences associated with the La Scala, Clydebank and those of others who have generously shared stories with me.

Hopefully this beautiful journey will allow readers to take a trip down memory lane and recall their own memories associated with the La Scala. It will take you through the good times, filled with fun and laughter, but also give an account of this great icon's sad times, which should never be forgotten. I'm sure that there will be a little something here for everyone, and a little nostalgic feeling about the past.

When you have finished reading this book, you will see that there are lots of questions relating to the information in this book. Why not try to see what you can remember of those times, dates and events?

I give you the La Scala, Clydebank.

Roger Clifford

Only a Bankie

There was a crowd standing in a queue outside the La Scala waiting to get into the bingo when a hearse drove by very slowly. To show their respect, the men took off their hats or caps. A wee elderly woman came away from the crowd and hobbled over to the hearse, placed a flower on it, before hobbling back into the queue.

Another woman said that was a nice gesture for her to do, to which the wee woman replied, **'Well he was a good husband, and we were together for 50 years'.**

The beginning, and end of an era

The La Scala was built on the hill off Kilbowie Road, informally known today as the 'Holy City'. Its grand opening was on Monday the 14 February 1938 (St Valentine's Day). It was opened by the MP at that time for Dumbarton Burghs, Mr David Kirkwood.

It certainly added a bit of glamour to the amenities of Radnor Park area.

In the coming years the La Scala cinema would be visited by

people from Clydebank and the town's surrounding areas and, indeed, from much further afield.

This beautiful building was made of steel, concrete and brick and had an art deco design. It certainly looked majestic, with its cream-coloured columns and dark coloured-glass entrance.

Picture 1: La Scala cinema

The tower of the cinema stood tall and elegant, with 'La Scala' displayed in neon, lighting up the landmark for travellers near and far. In Clydebank, it became as famous as the Singer's clock.

The Bankies loved it. These were hard working people, who deserved a little bit of leisure, and indeed, some luxury on their doorstep. But the cinema was also enjoyed by people from neighbouring towns and even as far afield as Glasgow, who came to gawp at its majesty.

The La Scala was closed in 1941 for three years, due to the ongoing war, and reopened in 1944 with this iconic structure managing to survive World War II.

On 31 August 1959, La Scala was taken over by Associated British Cinemas, better-known as the ABC chain and in 1965 it was renamed as the ABC. Sadly, the ABC closed on 12 April 1964 to allow conversion into a bingo hall, which was located in the former stalls, and a 776-seat cinema in the former circle.

It reopened on 31 July 1969.

The ABC cinema closed its doors for the last time on 19 February 1983, but the bingo remained open. A while after ABC cinema closed, the circle was converted into a snooker club. This eventually closed too, and in the mid-2000s, the Gala Bingo club also closed. A ban on smoking in public places, passed in Scotland in 2006, probably didn't help.

The great La Scala building lay empty for seven years, until 2006, when it was offered up for sale, by public auction, with an asking price of £100,000. Like most buildings from the same era, a lot of asbestos had been used in the construction of the La Scala. When the construction workers came in to demolish it, to make way for new flats, the asbestos was discovered, and work stopped for several months. Health and safety officers were called in and asbestos specialists had to carefully remove it, without releasing it into the atmosphere.

However, in 2016 the Clydebank Housing Association announced that a £5.1 million design and build contract had been agreed with A.S. Holmes (Scotland) Ltd. Funding of £3.168 million from the Scottish Government's Affordable Housing programme, came together with Clydebank Housing Association's own finance, to build 20 one-bedroom flats, 20 two-bedroom flats, and 4 two-bedroom wheelchair-adapted homes.

A sad ending to a GREAT CLYDEBANK GIANT.

A Piece of Nostalgia

From grans and granddads, to courting couples, short-trousered schoolboys and giggling schoolgirls, our thoughts and dreams will always remind us of this great, majestic picture house, the masterpiece that was, sitting on a hill in Clydebank … the La Scala.

Every evening without fail, whether sun, rain or snow, crowds would gather and form a queue to get inside and forget their problems, for an hour or two. The fresh smell of popcorn, the aroma pleasantly wafting down the aisles from the foyer. The glamorous, usherettes, with hair done up and seductive make-up, in their tight little uniforms, dishing out tubs of creamy, Wall's ice cream, Kiora orange drinks, Mivi ice lollies, Smith's crisps, and not forgetting KP peanuts.

There would be an endless din of chattering. Then, just like magic, the curtains would open, there would be a quieting hush, everything would go silent, lights down, and the huge Panasonic screen would light up. And then, what everyone

11

had been talking about for days ... The Movie. For the next two hours, you would be taken on an adventure.

Picture 2: La Scala cinema by Hugh Gillan

LA SCALA CLYDEBANK WHERE DREAMS WERE MADE ... HOW WE COULD WE EVER FORGET YOU!

CLYDEBANK ... Every Bankie, who lived from the 1930s to the first few years of the 80s, loved going to the La Scala. It was a part of growing up. It was a place to go with friends and a place to build relationships. Even in the 1960s and 70s not everyone had a TV (and certainly not a colour one!), so the cinema was a key place to watch the news. The audience

12

could hear what was going on in the world and see where the big events actually happened. Every workplace and playground in Clydebank murmured with talk about the latest movies. And after the weans had gone to school, neighbours hanging out their washing, would look over their washing lines and tell their pals of the great movie they'd seen with their man, with the words ... 'YOU HUV TAE GO AND SEE IT, HEN. GET YER MAN TAE TAKE YA'.

In the evening, taking the washing in, there was no time for talking or you would be late for eyes down at the Gala Bingo. If you won a line, you would be going home with a tenner. It was like you'd just won the pools. Aye those were the days ...

Setting the scene

New Town, Clydebank

Long, long ago, before the La Scala, or the Singer sewing machine factory was built, Clydebank was largely agricultural, and could be considered rural until the 1870s. As shipbuilding started to take off in the area, land was

13

needed. Along the River Clyde became a great place to build ships. Leading up to the 1890s, Clydebank was becoming more industrialised, and more populated, which resulted in it becoming a police burgh.

But the police burgh and town needed a name, so they took inspiration from the river, the Clyde banks (originally in what is Govan on the south side) and the name of the original shipyard, and Clydebank was born.

By 1885, the town was home to the largest factory on earth, Singer's sewing machine factory. It started with a modest 3,500 workers, but by the peak of its production in 1913, when it sent machines around the world, Singer was employing 14,000 workers.

Clydebank was firmly on the map and there it will stay.

Incidentally, shortly after I left school, I started as a young apprentice engineer at Yarrow's shipyard, just along from Clydebank on the River Clyde, where we constructed warship frigates for the Royal Navy. I was told by some of the older engineers that when the men were away fighting during the war, a lot of their wives helped to build the boats at Clydebank, and they were more of a match for the men. The majority of these women became excellent engineers, working in the engine and boiler rooms, even assembling the propellers, all with the precise calculations needed for this type of work.

Clydebank Blitz: 13–15 March 1941

Night of the bombs

Clydebank was bombed beyond recognition by German air power, the Luftwaffe, in two dreadful nights in March 1941. The German's main targets in Clydebank were the large factories, especially the Singer sewing machine factory and the John Brown shipyard, where boats were being built quickly to aid the Royal Navy in the war.

15

Houses, and indeed full streets, were completely destroyed during the Clydebank Blitz. The locals knew that an attack was planned on the John Brown shipbuilding, but being Bankies, they cleverly outwitted the Germans, and diverted most of the bombing by putting lights along Boulevard Road, which is now part of the motorway.

Picture 3: Night of the Bombs by Martin Kennedy

La Scala and the Blitz

The first night of the Clydebank Blitz, on Thursday 13 March 1941, a Shirley Temple film was showing at the La Scala.

But the great La Scala picture house stood tall, towering above all in Clydebank, and was untouched during those awful nights of the Clydebank Blitz.

16

In fact it was like a huge guardian angel, because it saved a lot of lives for those that remained inside the building.

It is quite amazing how the La Scala and the Clydebank Blitz are tied to many of these stories. Here are just a few of the stories people have told about their loved ones.

My aunt and uncle were in the La Scala during one of the nights of the bombing. When they eventually got to leave the cinema and come out, and seen the place flattened, all around them, it's a sight that always haunted them.

Others say …

My God, the stories of the Clydebank Blitz. Ma granny was blown into the Clydebank canal by a bomb blast, and ma granda had tae go in and fish her oot. He wiz soakin!

The La Scala picture house might have survived unscathed, but my granny's house had a direct hit, which blew the door of the air raid shelter, it hit her and knocked her clean out.

Picture 4: Child rescued from the rubble – Clydebank Blitz.

My mother was waiting to get into the La Scala shortly after the Blitz. She looked down along Second Avenue and could see that it was flattened. She then looked up at the poster on the La Scala cinema billboard, which read ... Gone with the Wind. *My mother remarked, 'Aye its gone with the wind all right.' I will never forget my mother saying that.*

Picture 5: La Scala after the Blitz

A Clydebank woman tells of how her mother was inside the cinema during a bomb raid on the town. When she was finally allowed out of the cinema by the wardens, who were trying to keep people safe, everything in the area around the cinema had been flattened.

In later years she told her family that when she made her way back through the rubble, her home was gone. The only thing that remained were curtains flapping in the wind through the windowless buildings.

Another Bankie tells how it was a miracle that more people

didn't get killed in the nights of the Blitz. Huge numbers of people sheltered from the bombs as Clydebank was blown to smithereens. Her twin aunties were about to go to the cinema but were not allowed out when the sirens started wailing. The sirens probably saved their lives, and the lives of many others on that fateful evening.

A lady recalls the story of her aunt, who was in the cinema during the Blitz. One of the Home Guard was standing at the doorway and told her that most of the streets had been hit by the German bombs, but they were now gone.

A Clydebank man tells how it amazed him how everything around the La Scala was flattened, and yet the picture house was untouched. During the nights of the bombing, the La Scala shook, and vibrations were felt throughout, but it stood, and was a safe haven for the people who remained inside.

Another lady tells her story of one of the nights of the Clydebank Blitz.

We were told to quickly go to Janetta Street, beside Clydebank High Park, where we would get buses to take us all away to safety. My sister and I were waiting in a queue for the buses to arrive, when the sirens went off, and there was a mad scramble for shelter. There were two shelters at either side of the high park. My wee sister and I were able to get into one of the shelters. Later that night I discovered that the other shelter had been hit by a bomb.

Another says:

I remember living in Crown Avenue and playing in the bombed houses all around us.

My sister and parents lived in Second Avenue, before I was born. A land mine was dropped by the Germans, and it dropped directly on our house, we lost everything. Fortunately the house was empty.

Evacuation to Renton. Very lucky.

Clydebank after the Blitz

Picture 6: Aerial view of Clydebank four years after the Blitz

During my time researching this book, I was pleasantly surprised with the many people who got in touch with me. They had great pieces of history about the La Scala and Clydebank that had been shared with them by a grandma, grandpa or someone older in the family, and they wanted me to share them with you.

La Scala remained like that until the1960s. I lived in this area from 1940–65 in four different houses; two in

Radnor Street, and Melford Avenue and Kilbowie Road. All can be seen in this photo. The area from Kilbowie Road to Singer Street, and Second Avenue to Crown Avenue, must have been about the most devastated area in the country, as only the La Scala and half a dozen houses remained standing; much of the devastated area had tenements.

Andrew R. McGhie

One gentleman recalls …

Did you know that the La Scala was crammed full of people's furniture after the Blitz on Clydebank? Most of it was never reclaimed. A lot of people had been killed, and others just evacuated, and never came back. My dad worked for the council. He told us that the furniture that was not reclaimed, after a period of time, was taken to Barnes Street in Clydebank, and was destroyed in what they called 'The Destructor'. These were very sad times for the people of Clydebank, as you will imagine.

Picture 7: La Scala sits on its own after the Blitz

Excerpt from *River of fire* by John Macleod

They're Coming Back

And so by daybreak, was all Clydebank – much of it still burning, entire blocks of tenements wrecked roads everywhere cratered or piled with rubble, the town everywhere reeking of burnt timber, burnt whisky, burnt rubber and – though few cared to dwell on it – the cooked roasting scent, here and there of human flesh. Scarcely a corner in Clydebank had been spared death; in some though the carnage was appalling.

On Second Avenue alone – where Janet Hyslop, keeking from the Radnor Park first aid station, had witnessed the bomb that 'pulled the face off Second Terrace' – 80 people were dead: they included ten of the Diver family at No 76 and eight Mc Sherrys at No 161.

On Pattison Street 43 had been slain: 31 on Dalmuir's Jellicoe Street: 27 on Napier Street: 23 on Radnor Street. (Including 9 of the Richmond family at No 60) 20 on Glasgow Road.

Courtesy of Birlinn Ltd, West Newington House, Edinburgh

La Scala Cinema

My first experiences (as a child)

As I was writing this book, I had a few stories of my own that I have included, which you might find amusing.

I was very young at the time, probably just started primary school. My mother and auntie wanted to see a film at the La Scala. I can't remember the name of the film, but my father, like a lot of fathers in those days, was working late, getting some overtime in to help pay the bills.

There was no one my mum could ask to look after me, as my auntie wanted to see the film too, so what did they do, well … They dressed me up like an old man and give me a five o'clock shadow, with a soft hat that nearly covered my eyes. It's amazing the things that you can remember from a young age and later in life become fond memories.

Anyway, my mum and auntie took me along to the La Scala. We were living in a house at 9 Hill Street, top left flat, which was quite near to the cinema. It didn't seem to matter what

26

time you went to the La Scala, there was always a big queue.

As we stood in the queue, Mum and Auntie kept me partially covered up, to the great amusement of onlookers. We seemed to stand for ages, and I wanted to sit down on the pavement, which of course I couldn't as I was to be a three-foot midget man for the night.

Picture 8: La Scala cinema queue 1953 (may have been queuing for ration books)

Picture 9: Interior of La Scala cinema

Picture 10: Foyer of La Scala showing columns

28

Picture 11: Interior of La Scala showing screen

Picture 12: Interior of La Scala – showing seating area

We did get in, me included, as I was helped by the women, with an arm each under my oxters, to look taller.

I was told afterwards that it was a good film, but that I fell asleep halfway through it, and that they were glad that they hadn't missed it.

It was tried again on another occasion, but this time I wasn't as fortunate, and we had to go home. My mother would remark years later that I would only have fallen asleep again.

Years later, this procedure would be practiced by my own family, which again turned out to be quite comical.

My wife, my older daughter, Alison, and I decided that we wanted to go and see a film in the new Empire cinema in the Clydebank Shopping Centre, but my younger daughter, Claire, was too young to take. She must have been about five or six years.

But like times past, my older daughter dressed Claire up, putting on bright make-up, lipstick, mascara, all the works, and just for good measure, a bra under her jumper. This was followed by a long coat, to make her look taller, that covered her small legs.

30

We told Claire just to keep smiling, with us walking in with her little body slightly raised off the ground.

I often laugh to myself when I think what the guy who was taking the tickets that evening must have thought when he saw this little baby-faced doll with bright lipstick and plastered mascara, smiling at him. I think it would be frightening … But guess what? She did get in … ate her ice cream and dozed off to sleep … just like her father.

Memories

I used to play football, with my mates outside the La Scala on Graham Avenue. We would put down our jackets, to act as goalposts, and enjoy a game of football, for an hour or two, until it got dark.

Little did I realise at that time that my son, Roger (Jnr), would also play football here with his pals when he was a little lad.

Climbing the La Scala

I was out looking for one of my daughters one evening when she was about 8-years-old. Now, Alison was a bit of a tomboy, and there was nothing she loved more than climbing. This particular time, she was on her own, and I heard a little voice shout, 'Dad, I'm up here.' I looked up and among the turrets at the side of the main front entrance of the La Scala, a little face smiled down at me. She was a dainty wee thing and had managed to squeeze through between them. She was happy, but I was terrified, the turrets were about 20 foot up.

I told her to get down immediately, but she couldn't. I had to scale up a good bit and managed to help her down. I can't tell you how relieved I was to get her back down to safety.

Dinner at the La Scala

I once took a flask of tea, and a bag of sandwiches in one afternoon. I told my son's teacher that I had to take him to the doctors. We fairly enjoyed that tea and sandwiches, as we watched the film.

I once took a kebab in with me; the smell aroused everyone around me and asked me if they were selling them at the kiosk.

Changed days from my old days in the La Scala. I would take a fish supper in after work when I got paid on a Friday. I now live in the land of Oz. We book recliner seats that come with the attached side table, where you can enjoy your pizza or whatever food you order on the side table.

Drunk going to the cinema

I used to go to the pub often to have a few beers, and then pick up courage to go to the cinema and look for the perfect woman. I never found one.

I remember having a few drinks before going to the La Scala, sometimes, maybe too much. I always fell asleep and missed some of the film. I could never tell anyone how the film ended but managed to get the last bus home.

I was drunk in lots of places around Clydebank, but kept sober in the La Scala, in case I got a lumber. I was quite small, so I paid half price on the bus going home.

Aye a wiz, many a time, and met up for a date, but its X-rated. What happened in the La Scala, stays in the La Scala

I took eight cans of Stella Artois in with me to see the film Troy.

I can't even remember leaving the La Scala. Someone told me later that two doormen helped to carry me out. I was well scooped.

I had a few good nights in the La Scala, back seats. Not many in the cinema. The memories are unprintable …

I remember about twelve of us getting a half bottle of Old England wine, before going to the La Scala. We were all very merry and laughed at all the saddest parts of the film.

I didn't drink much in those days. I was trying to keep my car on the road. I went one night to see the film, The Italian Job, *which included some great car chasing scenes. I always remember this idiot coming out of the cinema, and revving up his car, until smoke was burning off the rubber of his back wheels. Then he shot off down Kilbowie Road, like a bat out of hell. I think he thought that he could drive like the stunt drivers that were in the film.*

34

Picture 13: Eldorado advert

Big Skinny and the bogey

When Big Skinny was a wee boy, the craze around Clydebank was to build your own bogey (a cart made from a 3ft plank of wood to sit on, with string attached to the four pram wheels, so you could guide your bogey down a hill).

So Big Skinny makes his bogey, which he's very proud of. He takes it to the top of Crown Avenue, facing down Graham Avenue. Now Big Skinny has long legs, and his legs stick up when he is sitting in the bogey, so he decides to lie belly-down on his cart, to give him a better view of where he was going.

Off he goes down Graham Avenue, now it is a steep street, and he begins to pick up speed. Big Skinny tries to slow down, but then he remembers he forgot to put breaks on his bogey. In desperation he throws his two long legs out at the back, but by now the bogey is travelling like a bullet. He looks over to his left and whoosh he passes the La Scala cinema.

Some kids shout, 'Look at Big Skinny go. He's faster than the train going through Singer's station'.

In desperation Big Skinny points his two feet hard towards the ground. Smoke and the smell of burning rubber starts to arise from his sandshoes. Whoosh he goes straight down the stairs of Second Avenue and hits a row of bins in the back court, wedging himself head-first into one of the bins.

Twenty minutes later an ambulance arrives on the scene to take Big Skinny to hospital. What is the result? Concussion to the head. No sandshoes, and no toenails … Poor Big Skinny.

Was it haunted?

In the 1960s, my brother worked in the La Scala projection room, back where they run the film tapes and project them onto the big screen.

He used to tell me it was the scariest place to be, for the simple reason, that it was haunted. He told me that there were things that happened there were quite unbelievable. Once when he was alone in the projection room, a long-handled sweeping brush, which was lying against the wall, just suddenly flipped over and the shaft of the brush jammed against the feeding reel, causing it to snap. It was as if someone or something flipped the handle of the brush over to cause a scene or draw attention.

Another incident occurred with the cans that the films were delivered in. They were large, round and metal, with the length of the film determining how many of these cans there would be. This particular film had three spools of film, which had to be in the correct order of play. This would be checked out by my brother before the delivery guy, who delivered the films to the cinemas, was allowed to leave. This was common practice in cinemas.

When it was time to show the film, number one film reel was placed properly to start the film. When it was nearing the end of play, it would show a warning on the top right-hand side of the tape, to be ready to change to the second reel, and so on, so as the film would continue uninterrupted. Normally there were no problems and every evening, after the film was over, they would be stacked in order for the following evening. Before the next evening's showing of the film, the reels would be checked again to make double sure that they were running in order. This particular night, instead of the second reel coming on, the Pathe News *came on, interrupting the first part of the film. No one was in the room, apart from my brother, but the reels had been switched. No one else ever got into the projection room as the door was usually locked from the inside in case of any disturbance while the projectionist was working during the films. But somehow the films had been switched!*

He often told me things that happened there which just wasn't normal.

The Grey Lady

There's nothing to beat a ghost story to get your imagination going, and the projectionist isn't the only one to speak about there being a ghost or two in the La Scala. Here are a couple of the stories.

I started work in the La Scala bingo when I was eighteen. It was great fun, and everyone got on, but I'm sure that the La Scala was haunted. My mum had worked in the La Scala bingo before me and told me that there were strange things that happened that couldn't be explained.

Some locals swore that they had seen ghostly appearances of a woman dressed in grey. She never spoke, but drifted by them as if she was looking for something.

The story goes that the Lady-in-Grey was looking for her daughter, who was buried under the La Scala, or that her daughter's body had been put into the La Scala temporary after she died, then was removed.

I had a scary encounter one evening when I was cleaning up near one of the fire exits. I was walking backwards down the stairs and felt a light push and slipped. When I told the story to friends and customers, they said that maybe I was pushed, by the Grey Lady,

trying to get by.

Picture 14: Aerial view of La Scala,

Another lady who lived in Graham Avenue said ...

There was always a queue most nights outside the La

Scala. I was very upset when they pulled it down

because the Germans couldn't knock it down. I worked

in the La Scala as a cleaner when it was a bingo hall.

There used to be a ghost story of the Grey Lady who

had been seen on the back stairs of the cinema. As the

story circulated, newspaper reporters came to the La

Scala to check out the ghost story, and other people also

came to try and get spiritual readings. The La Scala held a lot of bodies during the war; it had been used as a temporary mortuary.

Battle on the Hill

It was evening – a nice summer's evening in 1965. The sun hadn't long gone down. The audience were waiting for the film to start. Some were teenagers on dates, cuddling up to each other or tentatively trying to hold hands, and were unaware of what was going to happen. Those who did realise what was going to happen, stayed alert and slunk down in their seats so that they couldn't be seen easily.

The film they were showing that evening was *Help!* with the Beatles. A Glasgow gang from Drumchapel were going to pay the La Scala Bankies a visit. Now the Clydebank boys knew in advance that the Drumchapel boys (known as the Drum Boys, or the Drumchapel Buck) were coming, so they were waiting for them in the cinema. When the Drumchapel boys landed, a great number were on scooters (which the mods used in those days), they kicked open the doors to the auditorium, shouting 'Drumchapel Buck, ya bastards'.

The Clydebank boys who were waiting for their arrival, roared back 'Come ahead.'

Then all hell broke loose ... gang warfare. There were bodies climbing over seats to get at one another. Both sets of gangs had weapons, known then as chibs (knives or razors used to stab or slash someone; also known as street blades). These boys weren't playing. When the doors at the back of the auditorium were kicked opened, a full-scale gang war broke out. The innocent by-standers were not expecting this. They screamed and stampeded to try and get out through the fire escape doors.

Screaming and roaring could be heard miles away but, going by the stories, the Clydebank boys outnumbered the Drumchapel boys. The fighting continued out onto Graham Avenue and then to the main road on the hill, Kilbowie Road.

The police did arrive, but they were not strong enough in numbers to control the young bulls that were bursting with testosterone and wanted war. It was said that the police just let the rival gangs fight it out and, when most of the fight was over, they jailed the bodies that were lying moaning in pools of blood.

I think it was reported in all the local newspapers the day

after 'The Battle on the Hill'.

One person gives their memory of that evening in the La Scala.

I remember it was in 1965, when I went to the La Scala to see the Beatles film, Help!

Halfway through the film, trouble erupted, and everyone ran to the front doors, but the front doors had been kept closed. My friend and I thought that we would be crushed with the crowd pushing to get out. Luckily the doors were opened, and we spilled outside the cinema, and a disaster was avoided, well maybe not, as a war was going on inside the cinema.

We never did see the end of the film ...

Some others said that they forced open the fire exit doors to get out.

One girl tells her story.

There was a stampede. I nearly fell and got trampled. I got up, took off my high heel shoes, and ran like hell to an exit door.

It was uncanny, but very appropriate that the film showing that evening was called HELP!

My dad was the doorman usher bouncer. Whenever he got the call he was there. He was there the night of the riot of the gangs when the Beatles movie, Help! *was showing.*

He never took advantages of anyone, but always gave two choices, 'Leave the easy way, or the hard way'. He put a few guys through the door without opening it. The gangs respected him … 'Fair but tough'.

While working on this chapter there was disagreement between the Bankies as to where the gang came from, some suggesting that they were from Maryhill, known as 'The Maryhill Fleet'. But I'm sticking with 'The Drumchapel Buck'! … What do you think?

Crying on a date

Here are a few stories about girls that went on a date to the La Scala and their boyfriends cried.

> *I was there as a boy and saw* Ring of Bright Water. *I had a lump in my throat, the size of an orange. I tried hard to hold back the tears.*

> *I went with my friend to see* The Last Snows of Spring. *After we left the cinema at the end of the film, we couldn't stop crying. We cried so much that the bus driver couldn't understand where we wanted to go. So we walked home still crying.*

> *I saw two drunks trying to climb the stairs to the balcony. They kept falling back. My sides were sore crying with laughter. How they got in I'll never know.*

> *This guy had the desert disease 'Wandering Palms'. He wouldn't give up till I hit him. He was quiet after that. I think he was quietly crying. Aye he cried alright after he paid for the tickets and meals at the end of the night.*

46

La Scala cinema curtains

Some of the older generation might have memories of the curtains showing the *Queen Mary*. Does anyone know where the curtains came from?

At one time the La Scala cinema had elegant curtains that closed in front of the screen at the interval and the end of the film. They were very special curtains. One might even describe them as majestic. One curtain had a print of the *Queen Mary* liner; the other, of New York skyscrapers. When the curtains were closed it gave the illusion of sailing to New York. It was awesome.

They were very beautiful but … I wonder if anyone knows where they ended up.

Dates, romance and love

When it comes to dating and romance the La Scala was an ideal place to go on a date. Here are some stories that might make you laugh:

> *One night I was taken to the La Scala cinema, on a date. Imagine my anticipation and excitement during*

47

the day knowing that I was going to the cinema with this boy who liked me. I kinda thought that he was cute too, and he had a car, which really did impress me, because not many had a car then.

This new date picked me up, in his car, and I felt quite the lady getting a chauffeur picking me up from my house and driven to the La Scala. We drove up beside the cinema and parked. The evening was going great, and at the end of the film, and we were all filing out, I thought to myself ... you lot have to walk home, but I'm getting driven home.

Now it happened to be quite a cold evening, but try as he might, he couldn't get the engine to start up, so he took a crank out of the boot to crank start the engine, but it still wouldn't start. Can you imagine my embarrassment? It seemed as if everyone was looking at him trying to start the car, and me, sitting all ladylike in the front seat, but freezing cold? When I now think back, it makes me laugh, great memories.

My older brother took me to every Doris Day movie at the La Scala, as he was in love with her.

My first date was in the La Scala, and he must have been the one for me, because it ended in him being my husband. I'm now married fifty-two years, and I'll never forget that first date.

I met him at the La Scala, dated him, married him, and then divorced him.

My first date was at the La Scala, when I was about fourteen. My mother would have killed me if she had found out.

I went to a date at the La Scala, to see a film called SCUM. *The guy was from Penilee. I never saw him again.*

I went on a date with my now husband to the La Scala. I fell down the stairs, from the balcony, broke the heel on my new sandals, and had to hobble home. I was absolutely mortified.

I took this girl to see what I thought was a movie called Flash Gordon. *It turned out to be a sex comedy, called* Flesh Gordon. *I don't know who was more embarrassed, her or me, but it was a good night.*

I went with my husband to see Guns of Navarone. *He slept through the whole film. Mind you, he was a bit sozzled.*

I took a girl to see Funny Girl; *I fell in love with Barbara Streisand. I bought the LP on the way out, but it was for me, shamefully enough. She never went out with me again, but I've had a lifetime in Barbara Streisand's company, even if it's only in music, and movies.*

I stood for over an hour outside the La Scala, waiting for what I thought was my dream girl, but it never happened, as she never turned up. Woe was me; I was broken hearted.

My date bought me a box of Maltesers, and guess what? I dropped them in the cinema, and they all went merrily ping ponging down the aisle, and under the seats. There was one left in the box, and he ate it. I didn't know where to look, it was so embarrassing, but I did get another date.

First date with my now husband, 50 years ago.

My first date at the La Scala was back in 1976, and there was a bomb scare. We all had to get out. Ruined date.

We used to go to the La Scala, and at the interval when the lights would go up, we would walk around the aisles, looking to get off with someone. I got lucky sometimes.

I went there with my boyfriend on our very first date, ended up marrying him, and lived happily ever after.

When I first went to the La Scala on a date with my boyfriend, I can't remember the film, but I cried throughout it. I was surprised that he asked me out again as I felt that I had made such a fool of myself. I thought that he would never want to see me again, it turned out he did, and we ended up happily married.

I remember going to the La Scala cinema, on my first proper date. I think it was a James Bond film that we were going to see. I happened to look around before the lights went down, and there, two rows behind me, sat my two older brothers. Date ruined!

I was going on a date to the La Scala and thought that we were meeting down the road at Singer's train station, but my date thought that we were meeting up outside the La Scala cinema. It was a bit of a mix up and the date fell through. I did bump into him again at a later stage, and we laughed at what had happened, but he didn't ask me out again.

The La Scala was definitely the social heartbeat of Clydebank, and a great place to take your girlfriend, or new date to on a Saturday night date. One of the worst things that I saw one Saturday night, was a guy and his girlfriend in the back seats. The guy suddenly became sick and had a vomit which projected about ten feet into the air.

Everyone was scrambling to get out of the way. You've never seen a half a dozen rows clear so fast in your lives, but I'm afraid some weren't fast enough to get out of the way, and it did hit a few.

The language that could be heard shouted out in the cinema, was really terrible.

The film My Fair Lady *was showing, and I went on a date with this guy. I knew within ten minutes that he wasn't the one for me, and the film wasn't great either. I made an excuse to go to the toilet and hopped it out the front door.*

I remember way back in the 50s we went to the La Scala, but the main attraction was to walk about flirting. We would walk around the aisles when the lights came up at the interval, to see, and be seen.

My husband and I worked there in the sixties. That's where we met one and other. We made a lot of good friends there, with the staff, and have some great memories.

I went on a date to the La Scala in the 60s. The boy smoked; I didn't. He asked me to try and smoke. I was reluctant, but gave in. On the way out going down the stairs, he passed his cigarette to me, and told me to take a large inhale. I inhaled alright, got dizzy then passed out! When I came around, I was at the bottom of the stairs, with people looking down at me, when I got up I saw two big holes in the knees of my black stockings. There wasn't a second date, and I never tried that smoking again.

I can't say that I had a bad experience in the La Scala, on dates, apart from boyfriends that used to have wandering hands.

Many a winch! I had in the La Scala when the lights went down!!

La Scala was one of the better cinemas in Clydebank, and if a guy asked you out, and suggested the Regal cinema in Dalmuir, you dumped him, because it was the pits.

Fantastic time at ABC Morning Minors when I was a wee girl. Then when I got older and met my husband, we would go to the La Scala to watch films when we could get babysitters.

The La Scala has to be remembered for thousands of date nights, and indeed many a wedding followed on from the romance.

There was a bomb scare on my first date ... Ruined. Then I had my wallet stolen on the way to see a film. Then my good watch was stolen, from Bruce Street baths. I was beginning to think that my luck wasn't great in Clydebank. I had enough, and decided it was time for a move. I moved to Canada in 1967.

Big Skinny's train journey

Big Skinny usually walked everywhere; that's why he was so skinny. But today he wanted to go on the train the one stop from Dalmuir to Singer's station. As the train was coming into the station, he hadn't time to pay for a ticket, so he quickly jumped on the train, thinking that he would pay at Singer's when he got off.

As the train approached Singer's station, Big Skinny noticed that it wasn't slowing down. In fact it didn't stop at all; on it went, straight passed the station. Someone shouted to him, because everyone knew him, 'Oi Big Skinny, this is an express train, it won't stop until Glasgow Queen Street.' Big Skinny could only sit there sweating as he only had the price of a ticket for one stop.

After about twenty minutes he knew the train was getting close to Queen Street Station, so he went to the nearest toilet for a quick pee. He could hear the train slowing down as he washed his hands and dried them, but something seemed to be wrong with the lock, and try as much as he could, he couldn't get it opened. In desperation Big Skinny shouted, 'Get me out of here. Get me bloody out of here.'

A passenger did get the door opened by forcing it from the outside, but it was too late as the train had started to pull out of Queen Street.

'What's the next stop?' shouted Big Skinny.

'Next stop is Waverley,' came the reply.

'Aw naw' Big Skinny said, 'that's Edinburgh.' But all he could do was sit back and look out the window as the train travelled through Glasgow and out into the countryside.

When he got off at Edinburgh Waverly, he explained to the ticket man what had happened. Thankfully, the man was very understanding, and let him through the gate, but Big Skinny had no money to get home. In fact, he just had enough for a packet of crisps, and this was all he had to sustain him as he walked all the way back home.

Not to worry, it only took him two days!

Poor Big Skinny, by the time he got back to Clydebank, he was very hungry, and his big banana feet were very sore, and to make matters worse he was now even skinnier than before.

La Scala poems

When I started writing this book, about this great monument reaching upwards towards the clouds, I felt that it was a straightforward piece of writing, about the facts, but as I progressed, the story sort of took me down different avenues, of sadness, romance, comedy. In fact it had everything. Then I looked at the poetic side of things, and soon I had an array of poems about the La Scala, so that the memory of this Clydebank icon will always live on.

Here is some work by local poets and artists.

A prominent Clydebank artist gives her following recollection of her La Scala days. Perhaps you can connect with her experience of the La Scala years.

Apricot-coloured Duchess by Lesley Jane Lang

> Satin swaggered curtains
>
> Choc-ices and Pearl & Dean

A Theatre of Dreams by Martin Hopkins

> Truly a theatre of dreams
>
> Where Fantasy, Horror, Action, and Adventure came to life
>
> Where on many occasions, I stood with a cast of hundreds,
>
> in a queue for an hour or more, up and around Crown Avenue
>
> Waiting anxiously to get in and seated.
>
> Just to see your heroes of the SILVER SCREEN

The Clydebank ABC by Hamish Mac Donald

> A flickering beam cuts through the years
>
> this memory spins between two reels
>
> a picture palace on a hill
>
> above a rainy working town
>
> where sat a fiddler on the roof
>
> and Eastwood gunned the bad guys down
>
> Where Moses led his wandering tribe

beyond the Holy City walls

I heard two thousand roaring weans

resounding through the packed out stalls

as Jason fought the skeleton host

or Tin Tin ventured far and wide

while Sinbad rigged his sailing ship

to journey up the River Clyde

Where sequels lived beyond the screen

when M had licensed Bond to kill

we hunted Blofeld and his gang

to chase them down Kilbowie Hill

as heroes put the world to rights

I lay my head to rest at night

as somewhere in a moonlit sky

a painted wagon trundled by

Then dreamed how King Kong swatted planes

while climbing towering shipyard planes

A Hard Day's Night (the legendary gang fight at the La Scala Cinema) by Hamish MacDonald

It's been a hard day's night
and the knives are out
it's said the Gilbie and the Buck
Clydebank's Capulets and Montagues
are bearing grudges and waging turf wars
The Fab Four are in town
as the crowd stretches back from cinema doors
then file in excited anticipation
but who sees the pack of wide-boys
lurking in the queue
The curtain parts
Pearl and Dean dispensed with
a guitar rings out the crowd cheers
It's been a hard day's night
John, Paul, George and Ringo
run towards a train station from screaming fans
A shout goes up
Gilbie ya Bass
they charge across the stalls
exchanging kicks and punches

malkies oot

And as adoring fans run towards the mop tops

The crowd in the cinema surges for the exit

Trampling Kia-Ora cartoons and ice cream tubs

Fast forward five years

and give peace a chance

King Kong Escapes (Clydebank ABC 1968) by Hamish
MacDonald

A cheer echoes through the auditorium

As Kong lobs a giant rock

Landing squarely

On the serpent of Mondo Island's napper

Then a fight to the death

Mechani-Kong, the evil robot creation

Half-blinding our ape hero

With rays from his mechatronic eyes.

Slugging it out

high on Tokyo Tower

that imposter Kong of Steel and our primal
champion.

The crowd unifies as one

a chant goes up

as we roar fit to bring down the plaster

King Kong! ... King Kong!

La Scala on the hill by Boyd McNicol

La Scala against a dark sky.

Searchlight strafing the dark, but the planes have gone

Flames light the distant clouds, and a washing line

Stepped pavements up the hill to red sandstone church

Pointy purple weeds thrive on the upheaval.

Massive concrete lintel broke, and orange rusted

Reinforcements poke out

Heavy steel beams over a moonlight canal.

Friday Cream Cookies for my Gran

Picture 15: La Scala on the Hill by Boyd McNicol

With a pocket full of pennies I always had to go

down to the great La Scala, to catch the latest show

it stood there on Kilbowie Hill, High, majestic in its prime

t'was a picture hall, built so tall, and well before its time.

As I rode there on a Saturday after queuing hours to see

the latest Masked Rider Show, with Zorro, the Green Lantern and me.

Each one of us we fought so hard and battled with the foe

then suddenly within this show would come Larry, Curly and Moe

The chuckles they had ended the battle had just begun the dangers they were imminent, and terror was rerun.

It was then the great Flash Gordon came, with powers so immense, soon put an end to the ruthlessness at these bully boys expense.

It was always here a pirate sneak would try and spoil the day, but a trusty shot, from a musket cocked, would wipe his grin away.

The lights went on. I looked around, and saw
faces filled with glee.

I holstered that wee gun of mine inside of me.

It wasn't long before 12 o'clock, when a man on
stage we'd see

'Whose birthday was that Saturday'. A gift in
hand had he.

A Minors Badge, a bar of choc, topped off with
corny jokes

He amused us all till we saw the ball

And sang that 'we're all pals together we're of the
Minors ABC'.

The Thrill at the Tap a ra Hill by Wolfman Bernie Logue

Saturday morning the excitement was of bliss

My friend Jackie Belshawe, to the Minors we
never missed.

Half a crown each for a badge and a ticket

Waiting for the usher to take the ticket and click
it.

With popcorn, drinks and lollies, and a bag of
Mars 'Treets'

We walked the dark aisles with the wumin,
onwards to our seats.

I remember they wore red aprons, and a band tied
in their hair

That torch they shone in our eyes, that was carried everywhere.

So patiently we waited, talking about last week's show

Shuffling arms with your mate, sitting elbow to elbow.

Warming velvet behind your knees, the sweat there made you irritated, and we leaned over the balcony to see what the film was rated.

We collected wooden sticks, from lollies with ice cream,

made a kind of 'Skyter' and chucked them at the screen.

Everything was dark, waiting for the start. Then the lights flickered, and Pearl and Dean played its part.

The adverts were long, selling ice cream and popcorn too

and showing clips of films then, the screen turned to a soft light blue.

The lights went back down again, like night-time, although we knew it was in the day.

Then a shout came from a cowboy yelling, 'Hi ho Silver, away!'

After that and a short cartoon, they had an interlude, but time was not quick enough, and the children became quite rude.

The ushers always told kids off, and we didn't want slung out,

but we always moved to different seats, so we didn't get found out.

Soon the main was over, we waited for lights up, we carried all our rubbish, and that was stuffed in a plastic cup.

We head up the stairway, making our way to the door, our legs were like jelly, as we stumbled on the thick carpeted floor.

The 'pictures' is what we called it, and they finished just around four, and did I fail to mention, both red light, and green light boxes, toilet and exit door.

We crashed through the exit doors, they were all around,

we always got lost in the crowd, but later each other we found.

Now sitting in darkness, makes you lose track of time

The cinema keeps you there very long, but everything is fine.

Your body and your head are tired, like heavy in the night, but as you breach the exit doors, we'll everything is bright.

Tribute La Scala memories

When I Was Young by Alex Doherty

When I was a young boy along I used to go

Down to the local pictures hall to watch the latest show

Buck Rodgers was my hero, he was a superstar as he flew along the universe, and mingled with the stars, but if there was a crisis or trouble, he would know and fly out to the rescue and defeat that dreaded foe.

Another of my favourites was Curly, Joe, and Moe, their antics used to make me laugh, until my sides were sore.

Detective Moe was funny, Joe and Curly too

Investigating robberies, and arresting people who they'd pursue.

They'd scramble round their local town, with silliness sublime

I fell about with laughter, at their efforts solving crime.

La Scala stories

The La Scala was the playground of my formative years, from running about daft in the dark at the Minors ABC, to smoking Woodbines in the dark, hands cupped over the lighted ends, so the usherette was blind to fact that the half price admission, only juniors were entitled to, were smoking, which was in the realm of the 16-year-olds.

Saturday night was for the big boys and girls in the Inbetweenies (ABC): too young for the pub, and too old for the Saturday matinee. Saturday night was chance of a lumber night! The ritual was passed down from the bigger lads to 'Novices' by example and a practised 'Casual Cool' promenade between the 'wee picture', *Pathe News* (cock-a-doddle-doo) and adverts (sometimes local). The trailers would give all 'Lumber Merchants' fair warning that the 'big picture' was imminent, and they'd better get seated near or next to the fancied one.

Picture 16: La Scala in its glory days

La Scala Enormous Satin Curtains Cinemascope by Red Down.

Green up-light provided a shimmering backlight to the silhouetted straggler in a light pencil skirt, white blouse with ruffles and enormous beehive (Ronettes Style) frantic to find ANY willing Ned to relieve her embarrassment. But things were about to get worse.

Out of the dark of the front stalls a twirling orange fag end found its target in the heavily lacquered beehive signalling the way for many more as the smouldering hive faltered screaming up the aisle well aflame.

Nobody took much notice. The big picture had started.

(Sent by Modern Telepathy Powered by Love)

Heydays! La Scala films and memories

One happy guy said ….

> *I loved the La Scala, I used to go there twice a week, in my teens. It was a great place. I remember queues going right around the block, for the film* GI Blues, *and the first in stereo was* West Side Story.
>
> *At that time it was probably the only place in Clydebank that had nice art deco architecture.*
>
> *The La Scala had a* Pathe News *film, which made everyone aware of international news.*

Another story was from a guy, who said:

> *I remember the queue for* Star Wars, *it went right up the hill from Graham Avenue, right onto Crown Ave. Those were fantastic times.*

I think that it was very sad that the building was neglected over the years, and finally demolished. It would have been amazing if the La Scala was rebuilt as a cinema down at the Clydeside. I know that there is a new cinema there now, but if a way could have got a way around this, it would have been a fantastic piece of nostalgia for the town.

One guy recalls the queue on the right-hand side was for the stalls. The queue, on the left-hand side, going down the hill was always for the balcony.

Another person recalls:

I think one of the last times I went to the La Scala, was to see Rocky 3. *The queue was horrendous. I somehow managed to bluff my way in, but hundreds got turned away.*

One other happy cinema-goer says:

I think it was one shilling into the stalls, but one shilling and sixpence up to the balcony.

74

Picture 17: La Scala programme Sept 1949 -

Another happy memory, from a lady:

I remember as a young child, being taken to the La Scala picture house, it was very plush inside. I didn't go often, but when I did, it felt so special.

I can recall on one trip, to the La Scala, being given a picture card by an usherette in the balcony area. It was a picture of a very glamorous Audrey Hepburn. I treasured that photo.

I can recall another time, when my mum and dad were desperate to see From Russia with Love, *so they took my sister and me with them, although we were still in primary school. We enjoyed watching the movie, and we also enjoyed sharing a box of Black Magic, what a treat.*

There was a downside to it, however, because my teacher was horrified to discover that some of my class had seen the movie. She said in one of those old-fashioned authoritative voices, 'Movies like that are not appropriate to see,' and she was most disappointed that any parent would even contemplate taking a child to see a film like that.

I also remember being taken to see West Side Story *with my mum and two aunts and getting a tub of ice cream during the interval. I always remember the wonderful clothes worn by the actors, bright scenery, fantastic dancing, and great music. The biggest surprise of the night was getting a big poke of chips on the way home. What a great night.*

Picture 18: Interior of La Scala programme Sept 1949

I went to the La Scala cinema about 1980 to see The Shining, *with the famous actor Jack Nicolson. My friends and I were fourteen. Great film.*

I remember seeing such classics, as Summer Holiday, *with Cliff Richard, and* Hard Day's Night, *with the Beatles, in the La Scala in the sixties.*

I loved the La Scala. As a young teenager, my friends and I used to sneak up the back stairs, to sit in the balcony. Once the film started, I would keep a look out, in case we were spotted. It was exciting and I felt a bit like a spy. I did it many times with my friends before getting caught, and we were flung out. When I went home I told my mum, that the movie was rubbish and we left early. Nobody ever recognised me, next time I went back.

I went once to the cinema; my dad took me to see Superman. *A few years later, I would go to the bingo occasionally with my mum. I don't think I ever won anything, but I did enjoy it.*

My friends and I always got thrown out of the La Scala cinema. After watching the film, we would try and stay on to watch it again. The staff got to know us and kept an eye on us.

Before the La Scala closed, I would meet up with some friends to play snooker in the upstairs snooker club. I always liked the dark smoky atmosphere in that snooker club.

The La Scala holds so many memories.

I might be wrong, but I think the last movie shown at the La Scala was ET. My wife was about eight months pregnant then. My son is now thirty-eight years plus.

I used to go to the cinema in the afternoon, and then nip up to the Hub disco when it was on at night. Great time.

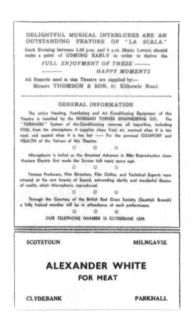

Picture 19: Interior of La Scala programme Sept 1949

I can remember when I went to the La Scala, with lots of other schools to see the original Oliver Twist, when it was circulating around 1950. It left a lasting impression on me.

I used to go to the La Scala on a Saturday afternoon when there were any Elvis films on. I was in love with him.

The first film my mum took me to see was an Elvis Presley film called Girls, Girls, Girls. It was a double bill, *and the second film was* That Darn Cat, *staring Larry Hagman. I think the time would have been around the mid-60s.*

Years ago my mum wanted to see the film Jaws *at the La Scala. She couldn't get a babysitter, but she managed to get me, then aged five, and my sister, aged seven, into the cinema. It wasn't a great experience, as you will understand at that age. My sister moaned, and cried throughout. Although I was very young I remember being so scared of watching this thing called* Jaws. *I was scared stiff. To make it worse, the music from the film also frightened me. Even now, years later, listening to that* Jaws *music, scares me.*

I have a memory of the Clydebank La Scala that I will always stay with me. There was a conversion of the La Scala in 1969: bingo hall downstairs and the cinema upstairs. At the grand opening night of the conversion my father took me to see Ring of Bright Water. *I felt so very important and proud to be attending such an event. I loved the experience so much that I started*

81

going myself to the cinema twice a week, to see whatever was showing. Unless it was a horror film, that was a definitely 'No'.

Many, many, years ago when I was quite young, I went with my mum to the La Scala to see and hear Frankie Laine performing some great songs. We enjoyed it so much, that we kept applauding, until the curtains came down.

I remember The Pathe News *so well. I used to like to stand up for the national anthem at the end.*

I remember as a youngster watching The Wizard of Oz *and the witch was the size of the screen. I was really terrified, and hid behind the seat in front of me, until she disappeared.*

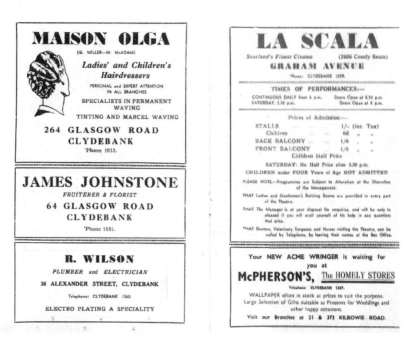

Picture 20: Interior of La Scala programme Sept 1949

I remember the massive queue, at the La Scala, when I went to see the film Help!, it seemed to go on for miles.

I grew up just across the street from the La Scala.

I grew up just across the street from the La Scala, and I went through different stages, where I went to the cinema with friends to see great films. Then I had a bash at going to the bingo with my mum, see if I could win anything. I was introduced to snooker with my dad taking me to the La Scala Crucible.

83

Went to see The Robe. *It was the first cinemascope in the La Scala.*

In 1976 the La Scala screened the great Bruce Lee star with his film Enter the Dragon.

Sad movies

My sister and I went to see The Last Snows of Spring. *It was very sad. We came out of the La Scala breaking our hearts, and both of us crying. We weren't the only ones; everyone in the cinema had a tear in their eye. I was sixteen at the time.*

I went to see Love Story *and balled my eyes out.*

I went to see the film Doctor Zhivago, *with my two sisters. They had to move to other seats because I was crying so loud.*

I went to see the film Soldier Blue. *I was crying and was so angry – those soldiers were bad guys.*

We were there to see the last film when the cinema closed. We took our son and daughter to see ET.

I remember seeing ET *and breaking my heart when he went home.*

I went to see the film Watership Down. *I broke my heart – there were dead rabbits everywhere.*

I went to see the film Shane *with my dad. It was so sad, I tried not to let him see me crying.*

I cried watching Bambi, *and* Love Story. *I went with my pal, and we both came out crying.*

Crying for other reasons

I hadn't much money, and I cried at the price that they were charging to get in.

I went to see a Norman Wisdom film, I laughed that much, I was crying ... crying with laughter.

Someone shouted 'Fire!' and we all charged out. I was wearing a brand-new jacket, and the pocket got caught on the seat, and all I heard was r ... i ... p and could see my jacket all torn. When I went outside I cried. I cried again when we went back into the La Scala, when we were told it was a false alarm, and that there was no

fire.

Saturday Morning Minors.

My wee sister and me at the ABC Saturday Minors

Picture 21: ABC Minors badge

Of all the things that I look back on in my childhood, I'm sure that the Saturday Morning Minors at the La Scala must be one of the happiest times in my life.

The ABC Minors had everything.

You see, in those days we didn't grow up as fast as kids do in today's world. Nowadays most children hardly leave their rooms; they have their computers, mobile phones, iPads, and TVs at their fingertips, and all this from a very early age. I'm not saying that's a bad thing – there's no holding back time. But we are progressing into the future at a fast rate, so it's nice to look back on simpler times. We might not have what kids have today, but it didn't hold us back.

We respected the older generation (sometimes) and appreciated that they were clever and astute.

I can remember it so vividly, going to the Saturday Morning Minors. I couldn't get to sleep on a Friday night just thinking about it, waiting in anticipation. Saturday morning would bring fun, singing, laughter and games.

I saved up quite a few Morning Minor badges and pinned them onto the lapels of my jacket. Felt so proud, as if I owned the place, I kinda thought that I was a quiet little guy, but realistically, I was no different from the rest, I was a little rogue. When I saw some others running up and down the auditorium isles, well I did too.

We used to collect ice lolly sticks. You were lucky if you had money for one ice lolly, but you were under seats looking for other lolly sticks so you could weave them together, and fire them, kinda like a boomerang. I always thought mine would go around the auditorium and come back to me, but it never did. Some of the other kids would fire them at the big screen, but I never had the courage to do that. If you were caught doing that, all your badges would be taken off you, you'd be put out, and told not to come back again.

Sometimes, my mother would give me two sixpences, one for me and the other to get my little sister Marian in, so that mum could get the housework and shopping done. Like the majority of Clydebank, in our home, Sunday was a day of rest. My mum was very house proud and would clean away into the small hours of Saturday night. I would often hear dad shout to her, 'Will you get into your bed,' well, that's another story …

With us at the pictures, Dad would go to the bookies to put on his Saturday horse line. Sometimes he was very lucky, and his winnings would take us on a Sunday outing to Rothesay. We'd buy the Sunday papers, which were always the *Mail on Sunday* and the *Sunday Post* (where I first started reading *The Broons* and *Oor Wullie*). Our dinner would be two big fish suppers by Rothesay beach.

I remember taking Marian to the La Scala, she couldn't have been any older than 5-years-old, and lifting her on a seat. Well, the seat was so high that her two legs didn't dangle over them, but just stuck out in front of her.

She never really left her seat and was always amused by whatever was on the big screen. I would keep one eye on the screen and the other on her to see that she was okay. Only occasionally she would get down from her seat and run with anyone that was running. I was so fly and could get away with it, but she was little and always got caught. I used to tell the ushers, who were going around with their torches, that she was my wee sister and that I'd look after her. I would buy her an ice lolly and tell her not to leave her seat. She was also given instructions to look out for any lolly sticks around her seat and keep them for me so that I could fire them.

Some Saturdays my mum and dad might say that they would take her shopping with them, but she would cry, saying that she wanted to go to the ABC Saturday Morning Minors, at the La Scala. She was learning, too bloody fast.

Sometimes, when I was on my own, I would hang back from the crowd going out of the cinema, pretending that I had lost something. When I was practically the only person left, I would go into the gents toilet and stay in one of the cubicles for a short time. When I heard people coming in for the Saturday matinee, I would come out and go through one of the auditorium doors that didn't have a person on it collecting the tickets. Most of the times, no one bothered checking me for a ticket and I got to see the Saturday matinee. But I would always make sure that I was home to see *Doctor Who*. The Daleks used to frighten the life out of me. I would imitate the Dalek voices when I was coming home from school. 'Exterminate. Exterminate' Those were the days.

Part of growing up

I lived at No. 7 Crown Ave, Clydebank, an area that everyone knew as the 'top of the hill'. It was just a stone's throw away from the La Scala, which was situated on the next street down on the hill, on Graham Avenue.

The tenement that I lived in had six families. Two apartments on the ground floor, two in the middle, where I lived, and two apartments on the top floor. There were thirteen children in that close, and most of them went to the Morning Minors on a Saturday.

Times might not have been great money-wise then, but you managed to get a sixpence off your ma, for your admission, and if you watched some pennies from during the week, you could buy some sweets before you went in. Our heids were well-buttoned on in those days.

Now, if there were thirteen kids in our close, with most of them going to the ABC Morning Minors, you can imagine how many were coming from other closes. In fact, kids came in their hundreds from neighbouring districts: Radnor Park,

Drumry, Hardgate, Duntocher, Faifley, Dalmuir, Old Kilpatrick, Whitecrook and Linvale, not forgetting Clydebank town itself, which in those days were bursting with families. Some even came from as far afield as Dumbarton and Partick.

Parents were never worried when they let their children go to the Minors. The cinema would look after the weans for the next 2–3 hrs. Mums and dads could get the shopping done, or the washing hung oot, getting school uniforms ready for school come Monday morning. Some children were younger than school age and they would trot along on a Saturday morning hand-in-hand with a big brother or big sister.

Typical dress consisted of warm tunics or coats fitted with waist belts, not forgetting the good old-fashioned balaclava, which nearly every child wore to keep their heads warm and protect them from the cold and rain. But the balaclava was very irritating and would have you scratching your head like crazy. I knew from experience on a Saturday morning that there would be queues and you had to get there early before the queue would extend up the hill and around the block. So the balaclava was a necessary evil! But it would be taken off and stuffed into your pocket as soon as you had made it through the cinema doors.

The La Scala doors would open around 9am and there would be an almighty rush to move forward. Lots of kids had their ABC badges proudly pinned to their jackets. Looking back at it, I realise what a lovely sight it was, to see such an army of children, happy and cheerful, talking about the favourite characters that they loved to see on the screen.

Eventually most of the children were inside, but it could take a little while. Sometimes there would be some singing, usually the ABC Morning Minors song, then the curtains would open and there was a deadly silence as the big screen lit up.

Not everyone sat in their seats during performance, and the management was constantly telling them to sit, not stand, on their seats. The most common remark was, 'Get back to your seats!'

It wasn't unusual to see two children sitting in one seat; I

93

suppose the management tried get as many folk in as they could. If you went to the toilet, you might come back to find your seat was taken, so you sat in the aisle, until you got another seat. Sometimes somebody wanted to swap a seat with you so that they could sit next to their pals.

The ABC Minors had a song that was sung every Saturday, sometimes a few times. You would read the words on the screen and would shout them out as loud as you could. Can you remember the song?

The ABC Minors Song

> *We are the boys and girls well known as, Minors of the ABC.*
> *And every Saturday all line up*
> *To see the films we like, and shout aloud with glee*
> *We like to laugh and have our sing song*
> *Such a happy crowd are we*
> *We're all pals together*
> *We're Minors of the ABC*

Sung to the tune of 'Blaze Away' by Abe Holzmann

Halloween party

I had many happy times with the La Scala Morning Minors.

One of those times was a Halloween party. Incidentally there were parties for everything at the ABC Morning Minors.

Anyway this was a Halloween party, and there was a costume contest. Now my background wasn't poor, but we weren't rich either, looking back we just about kept our head above the water. Anyway, I wanted to dress up. Now my father was a real character and could tell a good story that kept your concentration; but my mum was the artistic one, with natural creative skills. She was great at designing and painting things to make them stand out. Anyway she told me that she was going to make me into a very old man.

Firstly she cut up old trousers, shortened them and put braces on them, then a collarless granda shirt. She fixed an old white handkerchief around the contour of my face, cutting out pieces for the eyes, nose and mouth. She then made a wig out of hair buns and made me bushy eyebrows and a moustache, which was glued onto the facemask. Then the face had to be lined with a pencil. Even though she was working with so little, the effects were fantastic. Finally, I was given a small walking stick. The rest, she told me, was up to me. I had to act the part, which I did, and shuffled about as I walked.

Saturday morning came and I got dressed into my costume and off I went, with my perfected shuffle to the cinema. There were lots of other kids all dressed up: one boy in a Superman suit; another as Batman; and a very good, Little Red Riding Hood. The more that I looked at the kids who were dressed up, the more I thought that I might not be the win.

In between the films that morning they had heats for the competition. To begin with, the stage was packed, but we were whittled down until there was no more than eight of us.

The judges finally chose a boy and a girl as the winners, and guess what? … Yip, you guessed it … I won first prize … a huge tin of Quality Street.

That was a big prize in those days, and I was so proud. I think this was the first time that the actor in me was beginning to emerge. Not long after I left school I joined the

Clydebank Repertory Theatre.

When I got my prize and came down from the stage, I ran out the doors and home as fast as I could with the prize stuffed up under my shirt. I was afraid that I would get ambushed for my sweets if some of the others saw that I was on my own. When I got home, I showed my mum and dad and sister what I had won. My parents were really proud of me, but my little sister was more interested in eating my sweets. I did hide them, and she did find them (I noticed that they were slowly being pilfered). Now that's another story. But she could get away with murder as my dad always took her side. She was his 'Little Blue Eyes'.

Easter bonnet

The same happened when there was a contest for the best Easter bonnet. My mum made an Easter bonnet for my little sister. You might say to yourself that it was easy to make, but have you ever seen an Easter bonnet with little chicks trying to fly out of the bonnet from a nest attached to very fine wire? It was very cleverly done. She also won first prize, more chocolates. I was her bodyguard home, and I helped her to eat her chocolates. Well, I was her bodyguard! Of course I had to get paid in chocolate.

Ol' Blue Eyes belts it out

I also won a singing contest at one of the ABC Minors. I was picked from a few heats to go into the final. The contest was to see who could sing the Minors' song, but giving it a little action. Guess who won it? 'Yip, Ol' Blue Eyes, with the snake hips'. I never quite lost the slippery, shaky, hip routine!

Other Minors have their say

I have gathered together some stories from other people that I'm sure you will not only relate to but will also put smile on your face.

> I went to the Saturday morning ABC Minors, in the La Scala, with my siblings. I loved running up and down the aisles, and buying things like 'Everlasting toffee'. Oh happy days. It was a sixpence to get in. I think my mum thought it was worth it, to get a few hours peace.

Another happy ABC minor, says:

I used to go to the Minors, every Saturday morning, sometimes the queue was so big, and you had to queue right around the La Scala building. Then when you got in, you would run up the winding staircase, quickly get into a seat, and get ready for the films.

If anyone had a birthday, and the staff found out, they would drag you up onstage, and everyone sang 'Happy Birthday' to them, and you got a goody bag. I think that I can remember that some of the fly kids had a few birthdays throughout the year.

I was an usherette in the La Scala. I hated being on the Saturday morning ABC Minors. The weans were mental.

There were a few of us, and didn't have much, so one paid in, and then they went to the fire exit door, opened it and let us in, and others got in as well.

When I was a little girl, going to the ABC Minors, I use to love it when the cowboy John Wayne and the cavalry came to attack the Indians. Everyone would shout … 'Easy …easy …easy'.

On a Saturday morning when going to the Morning Minors ABC, I would use some of my pocket money, seven and a halfpence, to buy sweets from R.S. McColl's newsagent at the top of the hill. You would get a variety of sweets there for your money.

When you got to the cinema, sometimes they had set up a model train set, just outside the auditorium. It was great watching it travelling around the track, going through the tunnels, but you were never allowed to touch it.

I myself have fond memories of that lovely cinema.

Picture 22: View from Kilbowie Road along Graham Avenue

My auntie's friend worked there, and she would give us free entry for helping her out in the kiosk.

I used to collect all those colourful badges that were taken off the kids during the interval for running around wild and not staying in their seats.

When I went to the ABC Morning Minors, I used to take sweets with me. One Saturday, I took a bag of soor ploom sweets. They were great. I was enjoying them when one stuck in my throat. I couldn't breathe! Luckily my friend was with me and thumped my back until it came back out ... Boy wiz I lucky. My face was like a red balloon.

I went to the ABC Minors one Saturday morning and took a very sore head, a migraine, that came on quite suddenly. I was taken to the doctor's surgery, which is now Jon's hairdressers, at the top of the hill on Kilbowie Road.

I used to have an ABC badge, and if you were lucky, they asked you to go up on the stage, for five minutes of fame. To sing the songs, you had to follow the bouncing ball.

I used to love the Saturday morning ABC. After a cowboy flick, I used to run home, well actually ride home on my horse, whacking my thighs, and shooting any injuns that got in the way. Those injuns would have been neighbours. The neighbours probably thought that I was off my head.

When I was young, a gang of my friends from Holly Street and I would all go to the ABC Morning Minors. After it was over, we had fun re-enacting the scenes from the movies on our way home.

There were always lots of chances to win a Morning Minor badge. Some would dance to win a badge. We all had great fun, and not a parent in sight. If my memory is correct, I think it was sixpence or a shilling to get in. I'm also sure that they would take empty jam jars to get in.

One lady, now living in Canada said:

I was very young when I started going to the ABC Saturday Morning Minors, and I think it cost about ten pence to get in. At the start of the Morning Minors, you had to sing all the songs. Then we enjoyed the cartoons that were put on. Flash Gordon, *the superhero, was on a lot at the ABC Minors, and used to get all the children cheering when he would win against the evil enemy.*

During the interval, the cinema attendants would find it difficult, to get the kids to sit in their seats, and stop running up and down the aisles. Sometimes there were competitions, where you could go out to the front and dance to the latest music. Now this is where you could win an ABC badge, to pin on your jacket or coat. Also children who had a birthday on that day, or that week could win a badge. There were letters that you could save up to make ABC MINORS. Well, WOW! Then you got a large posh badge.

Picture 23: View from Singer's train station, Kilbowie Road

The main movies were British-made children's movies. At the end of a movie there would sometimes be a treat, and that would be a Disney cartoon. Some of the cartoons on display were Bugs Bunny, Popeye, Looney Tunes and a host of others. The Lone Ranger and his side kick Tonto were on nearly every week.

Another ex-Morning Minor, says

I was always desperate to find out the following week if Flash Gordon had survived yet another impossible situation. But he always got out of it, only to get into another impossible situation. I paid an extra three pence to go upstairs. I used to collect ABC badges and loved how they would glow in the dark.

I used to go every Saturday morning to the ABC Minors, when I got older I went to the cinema to see all the classic movies, until it got closed down. After that, it was up the stairs to the Crucible snooker hall ... Aw memories.

I used to run down into Clydebank town centre, slapping my hips, and pretending I was riding my horse after watching cowboy films at the ABC Morning Minors. I used to think I could go faster if I slapped my hips. It's now so funny thinking back.

I used to go to the Morning Minors on the Saturday morning, and then went horse riding up in the Cochno farm, in the hills above Clydebank in the afternoon.

I remember Zorro, *and* Five on Treasure Island. *It was great then.*

First time I saw King Kong, *it shit the life outta me.*

I remember queuing up to get in; I didn't care what was on, whether it was Lassie Come Home or Zorro, as long as I got in.

It was the dancing at the end that I loved when we were rewarded with an ice lolly.

Down the two outer aisles, there were pillars, which stuck out a bit. While larking about, I ran smack dead centre into one of the pillars. I then saw stars, but it wasn't on the big screen in the cinema.

A crowd of us used to go to the ABC Minors on a Saturday morning. I was sitting waiting for the film to come on, and I heard someone shout my name. I quickly turned around and was hit by an empty ice cream tub that someone threw. I got it right in my eye, right in the kisser. Tears started screaming down my cheek, my eye started smarting, and I didn't enjoy any of the films that day.

I got hit with a boomerang of ice lolly sticks once, which the bad boys were throwing. It skirted of my

*head. I thought the hair had come of my head. Yip …
the good old days?*

*I remember going to the Saturday ABC Minors with
my brothers to see* Dumbo, *the flying elephant. Years
later I went back to the La Scala to see* Saturday Night
Fever, *starring John Travolta and Olivia Newton John
[sic], when I was only fifteen. I can't remember the
rating, but I might have been too young.*

One well-known Bankie told this story.

*I used to look after the kids at the ABC Saturday
Morning Minors. I used to walk around in my La
Scala uniform, shining a torch along the rows, and
telling the kids to keep their feet off the seats.*

*I went regularly on a Saturday morning for a couple of
years. I don't remember ever getting a badge. I think
they were given out when it was your birthday, but I
was a bit shy to go onto the stage and collect one. You
also sometimes got a small gift. Those Saturday
mornings were really busy with both the stalls and*

107

balcony packed with kids. From memory it was sixpence (old money) in the stalls, and ninepence upstairs in the balcony. The added benefit of being upstairs is that you didn't suddenly get hit with an empty ice cream tub carton on your head, chucked from above. But it was great, back in the day.

I remember buying a badge but don't remember how I got it!. Loads of great memories, watching Flash Gordon, *and singing the Minors song. My brother and I would get the train from Dalmuir train station, and pretend it was Flash Gordon's spaceship.*

I loved all the children's films in black, and white. Only thing that spoilt going to the Saturday Morning Minors was that there were sometimes little gang fights. It's just as well that I was a very good runner then.

I loved it when the lights went down, and you watched the film in the dark. I hated when the big bright lights came on. Sometimes you got a piece of cake if it was your birthday.

My big brother collected empty lemonade bottles and would give them in at the cinema to get us to see the films. I did once get a badge, but for the love of me I can't remember how I got it.

We didn't have much money in those days; we couldn't afford to go the ABC Morning Minors. We had to help with the housework.

Looking back I would have loved to have gone, but I was really shy in those days, and didn't go.

I'm now a lot older, but I can't remember how I got my badge, but I do remember it glowed in the dark, magic memories. I wore my badge every Saturday morning. I didn't like the guy that always growled at you, with the wine-coloured jacket. He always had a growling looking face. Then it was dancing at the interval. The best dancers got an ice lolly. I was the top twister dancer. I used to get shouted up to the stage. I was very popular for a few weeks. Loved going every Saturday morning.

We used to stamp our feet when Flash Gordon came on and fought the Clay men. We would shout at the top of our voiced 'Eaaaasy. Eaaaasy'.

I knew Jack, the man that showed you to your seat, at the ABC Minors. I think he was a big child at heart himself as he had a big model railway in his house. He was a great guy.

I used to go with my little brother, on a Saturday morning, 9am 'til 12 o'clock. We took a sixpence to get in, and we had a Curly Wurly chocolate and an apple each. I used to love the singing before the pictures started. There would be a man on stage who would split us into groups, 'Left' or 'Right', or 'the balcony' versus 'the stalls'. We would sing the ABC Minors song and see who could sing it the loudest.

OMG!! ABC Minors every Saturday morning. Boys versus the girls. It was an enjoyable riot ... Fab days.

We all had great Saturday mornings at the ABC Morning Minors in the La Scala. It was more like a theatre morning, with a compère keeping the

110

entertainment going, and everyone joining in, and all that movie action. Ahh the ABC Minors, who was the guy with the jet pack on his back? I'm thinking he was something like Captain Cody. The guy would be halfway off a cliff in a car! Definitely no chance of survival. You'd be left in suspense of what could happen. Then you'd go the next week, thinking, 'he's deid,' but miracles of miracles, he didn't die, he made it, and the car was now nowhere near the cliff. How did we all fall for that? Every week there was a cliff hanger, but naybody died.

ABC Morning Minors has brought back some memories. My sister and I loved the Minors every Saturday morning. My sister has often said that she is an ABC Minors wean. I tried to introduce the same idea to our local cinema in Inverness (with a little success) those were the days.

Saturday Morning Minors, five pence in, and if you took a birthday card with you, then you got in for nothing. Great times.

ABC Minors Saturdays. Those were the days. Although those square tubs of orange were just coloured water. No taste!

My sister has the ABC Morning Minors ringtone on her phone.

Good times. It was the pictures then the baths on a Saturday morning. How lucky were we?

Making lolly stick boomerangs, firing them at the screen, and the monitors trying to find out who did it.

I remember saving up the ABC badges, and sometimes swapping them if you had two badges that were the same.

I got my pocket money on a Saturday morning. Two shillings. I had money to get in, to the ABC Minors, buy sweets, and I had money left over.

I remember when it reopened after a facelift to the place, and it showed the film Ring of Bright Water, *and an otter was brought along!*

A wee memory about the badge as I remember it is (might not be 100% accurate, but not far away). Every time you attended on a Saturday morning you got a 'wee' badge with a letter on it (might've been free?). All the letters spelt out 'ABC MINORS'. The thing was to get them all to spell ABC MINORS, and once you had them all and proved it to them, you got the big one, as pictured. They would write your name on a piece of paper and stick it on the middle of the badge, that's long gone now but you can still see the Sellotape marks. It was literally a 'badge of honour' to display the 'big one' on your jacket, lol....

Picture 24: ABC Minors badge

Outside La Scala

I had my motorcycle stolen twice from outside the La Scala when I was inside watching a film. On both occasions it was recovered in Drumchapel.

113

I'm not sure what was ever on at the La Scala, but I do remember playing football in the gravel car park at the back and side of the cinema. The funny thing was, there were never any cars parked in it. We used to play wally against that massive wall. We were young, and we never thought how old the La Scala was.

I remember picking sides with my mates for a wee quick game of football outside at the side of the La Scala. Then the manager would come out and shout to us to clear off.

I always thought that it was funny that the La Scala car park never had many cars in it. Anyway you couldn't have a great game of football in it as the water-filled potholes spoilt a good game.

The La Scala should have been kept as a museum.

Picture 25: Looking south onto Graham Avenue

Big Skinny gets well and truly tanned

One morning Big Skinny got up and looked at himself in the mirror. 'I'm awfy peely wally', he said to himself. 'In fact I'm as white as a ghost.' He looked out the bathroom window and saw that it was a real nice sunny day.

So nice a day, that some cows had come down from the hill and had wandered into the back courts where people had their washing hanging out. As Big Skinny watched, two cows were having a good munch on wee Mrs Murphy's bedsheets.

'Go away cows' he shouted. 'Shoo, go on, go away cows,' but they took no heed of him, so Big Skinny left them to it.

Then he thought that it would be the perfect day for sunbathing. So he got his rucksack out and started to pack it. In went

115

a small bottle of water, sunglasses, and a packet of crisps just in case he got hungry.

He put on a very colourful shirt and a pair of tight shorts, with legs that could be tucked up, so that the sun would get to his milky white chicken thighs. And topped his outfit off with a straw hat and a pair of pink plastic sunglasses that he had found.

He set off and soon he was walking past the Goldenhill area, where there was a crowd on the corner.

'Where are you going today?' someone shouted.

'I'm going to get suntanned,' Big Skinny shouted in reply.

'Well don't forget to put plenty of suntan lotion on. It looks as if it's gonna be a toaster.'

'Damn it,' thought Big Skinny, 'I forgot the bloody suntan lotion. Well, I'll just need to be careful.'

Big Skinny walked to Dalmuir Park then looked for somewhere quiet and private to sunbathe, but there were people everywhere. Then he saw a place, a little island where the only inhabitants were the ducks and swans. 'Ah ha,' thought Big Skinny, 'that place will be ideal.' So he climbed the fence, jumped into the water, and waded through until he got onto the island. The ducks and swans weren't too happy with him, but Big Skinny didn't care, he had found a great wee place away from everyone for some serious sunbathing.

It seemed like he had only closed his eyes when he heard a voice shouting.

'Hoi you!'

Was he dreaming? Then he heard it again, only louder.

'Hoi you,' was followed by a loud whistle sound. 'You, the big skinny guy!'

Now Big Skinny definitely knew that he was the one that the park keeper was shouting at.

'Get out of there! It's private! Get out or I'll phone the police!'

Big Skinny waded back to the other side of the bank, but he realised that his whole body was very sore. When he looked at himself, he was as red as a beetroot. 'Aw naw,' he must have been sleeping longer than a couple of minutes, and with no suntan lotion on. The only part of him that was white were his eyes, as he had been wearing his pink plastic sunglasses.

Big Skinny felt more like a big drip, walking home with a bright red face and two big white eyes.

Memorable movies

A new era of films was starting to emerge in cinemas, and one of the first must surely be *Star Wars*, which hit the big screen of the La Scala, Clydebank in 1977.

It certainly was a turning point, from churning out meaningful stories of dramatic conflict, to a completely different type of film sprawling with special effects that had not only the children mesmerised with the special effects but the adults too. With the movement of spaceships sailing in intergalactic space through the stars and the weird and wonderful creatures from other galaxies, some more advanced and with greater intelligence than us Earthlings. Yes, this was a dawning of the new age of cinema.

The special effects and out-of-this-world ideas, combined with advanced cameras, with inbuilt new technology, had you gripping the arms of your seat with that uneasy feeling that at any time you could be zapped by a laser gun. Just imagine being taken out by a zap of colourful light … What a way to go!!!

118

Some stories that I have to give a mention to are by a Clydebank guy who said:

My friends and I went to see this Star War *movie, when it came to the La Scala in 1977, and see what all the fuss was about. We were always quite a noisy lot, but there wasn't a noise of any sort throughout the film. I was memorised by the special effects, as were my friends. When I looked around the cinema, everyone was eye glued to the screen.*

Grease 1978

I recall the long queues waiting to get in to see the film Grease. *The guys and gals were all dressed up in their* Grease *outfits, looking brilliant. Then during the interval, they got up on stage and started dancing. It was brilliant; I'll never forget it.*

I remember as a kid, my sister and her friends being forced to take me to see Grease, *because I wanted to see it. My sister wasn't happy at all, because she had to take me, her little brother.*

119

I didn't get to see Grease *and cried all the way back to Linvale with my big cousin.*

I remember when the film Grease *came out, the queue to get in was massive, I never thought that I would get in, but I did. I love that film.*

I went to the ABC Morning Minors every Saturday morning without fail, and loved it, and all the songs. Everyone tried to sing louder than anyone else. Later as I got a bit older, my friend and I went to see John Travolta and Olivia Newton John in the musical Grease. *We loved it so much we went back to see it eight times. We sang out every word of all the songs. We kept being shouted at by the audiences who were there watching it to 'SHUSH IT'.*

I couldn't see what all the fuss was about it.

Sharing memories

Picture 26: Interior of La Scala screen showing information about CYAB

Call yersel a Bankie! (CYAB) has a Facebook page with over 28,000 members and growing! Find out more at https://www.facebook.com/groups/clydebank

The local area

Two great shops on Radnor Street, Clydebank

If you know a little bit about the history of Clydebank, you will know that at the top of Kilbowie Road (known as 'the top of the hill') there is a street called Radnor Street. Like most of Clydebank it had been severely bombed and most of the street had been flattened. As a child I used to play amongst some of the ruined buildings. There was only a small part of the street, nearest to Kilbowie Road, that was not too badly damaged.

There were a few shops, a chemist and a pub (Cleddans Bar – that still stands to this day, on the corner of Kilbowie Road and Radnor Street). There was a bookmaker down Radnor Lane off Radnor Street; I'm sure it was called Walkers.

But there were two shops that practically every Bankie will remember … they were Billy Bellingham's Newsagent and McNaughtan's Chippy.

Picture 27: Radnor Street: Billy Bellingham's Newsagent and McNaughtan's Chippy

Billy Bellingham's Newsagent

I remember when I was no bigger than knee high, we moved from 9 Hill Street (one end of the street had been bombed during the war), to the newly-built tenements and 7 Crown Avenue.

My dad, who has the same Christian name as me, Roger, would send me on a Saturday evening to Billy's for a packet of razor blades. He always liked a close shave, before putting his shirt, tie and suit on and going out for a few drinks on a Saturday evening. After all, he worked in the construction industry where he always wore overalls and

123

leather boots, with steel toe caps, so a few drinks with fellow workers was much appreciated.

My mother never really drank alcohol though, on the occasion, she took a wee sherry. It was always quite funny because her face would go bright red. Like a lot of mums and housewives of that era, she was very house proud, and would clean the house until you could see your face in the carpet!

I was often in Billy Bellingham's shop. Billy had two ladies who worked alongside him, one was Mattie, his wife, the other Lorna, their friend. Billy sold everything from newspapers, to confectionery, to small gifts and indeed anything you couldn't get in the chemist, Billy had it.

Billy's always had good custom, every day, every week, from schoolkids coming into his shop during lunchbreaks and at home time to get their sweets and crisps.

On the rare occasion when I wasn't feeling too well, my mum kept me off school and would pop into Billy's for the *Dandy* or *Beano* comic, to cheer me up. I also loved *Roy of the Rovers* comic, and I'm not ashamed to say it, but when my young sister would finish with her comic, *Lady Penelope*, I would read that too.

During my Morning Minor days, I would go to Billy's first to buy my sweets. Billy's could give you a far better variety of goodies to choose from than the La Scala provided. Some Saturday mornings there would be a queue to get served, with trays of sweets laid out for you to choose from. Personally I loved Mars Bars, and toffee, and I would get them at Billy's.

As I grew a little older I might be in Billy's in the evening and I would see couples coming into his shop to buy chocolates, then hurriedly dash off to see the film that they had been planning to see all week.

One lady tells of such a vivid memory from when she was young …

> *Omg it brings back memories. I lived around the corner at 377 Kilbowie Road. I remember buying Christmas presents for my family at Billy Bellingham's. Cigarettes for my dad; Palmolive soap,*

with free plastic pearls for my mum; and a quarter of sweets for my gran.

I also used to go in there to buy MB chocolate bars, and sweets on my way to school. I loved Billy's and have so many memories of it.

I hope these stories bring back your own memories.

The Best Wee Chippy on Radnor Street

My memories of Mc Naughtan's chip shop again started very young. One of the ladies who ran the shop was a lovely lady of the name Mary Milne. She often served me chips and sometimes used to ask me if I had any old newspapers, which were used in those days to wrap up your chips or suppers to keep them nice and warm until you got home. Sometimes you could read a story from the newspaper on your way home. If you took newspapers into the shop, you always got a lot of extra chips. I'm not exaggerating but sometimes when you opened that bag there were enough chips to feed a family of ten hungry weans.

My mum would sometimes send me to get chips to put with our salad, or to add to a meal on our dinner plates.

As a schoolboy, I would sometimes be standing in a queue inside McNaughtan's shop when a fight would break out (it was a good place for adolescent boys to settle scores). Everyone would stand back as fists and feet would fly, but Mary would lift up the hatch of the counter and come out to somehow break it up.

'Behave if you want to be served' she'd shout, 'or get out and fight outside.'

Mostly the row would be over, and chips and suppers served to all.

As I grew up, I used to go the La Scala during the week with the films usually finishing about 10pm. Then, I would run up Kilbowie Road to McNaughtan's, to get a bag of chips before it closed for the night.

I remember Saturday nights well. My dad would go out for a few beers to the Cleddans Bar, which was only a hand's throw from McNaughtan's. So on his way home he would go in for a fish supper and a bottle of orange juice for my mum. He would quietly open our front door, and quietly close it again, not to waken my young sister or me. But I'll tell you, the beautiful aroma of that fish supper would raise Lazarus from the dead. My little sister and I were like two greyhounds charging up that hallway to get a share of that delicious food.

Many a poor soul who would leave the Cleddans Barr at the end of the night not too good for wear or tear from the alcohol and would go into Mc Naughtan's for chips. Mary Milne would sometimes throw in a fish alongside the chips, knowing that it was probably the only meal that they had had all day.

A lady told me recently that if you wore your Brownie uniform in, some evenings you would get your chips a little cheaper.

A gentleman told me that he once bought a fritter supper from McNaughtan's chippy, and he read the date and name of a local Clydebank guy who was going to court the following week.

I'm sure that many of you will have memories of McNaughtan's or your own local chippy to tell.

Vet at the La Scala

In the 50s, maybe the 60s, an ex-army 3-tonne vehicle, which was rigged out as a veterinary surgery and run by the SSPCA, would park beside the La Scala most Wednesdays and treat the animals for free. Most people left a donation though.

Wedderlea Dance Hall

When I was looking for stories for my book, I was told that there was a dance hall directly across the road from the La Scala, on what is now Graham Avenue. I was intrigued to find out more about this as I had heard that a bomb hit the hall during the Blitz.

I made enquiries, but heard nothing more about it, and then I received some information from a gentleman who not only knew about the Wedderlea Dance Hall, but his family built it. I now give you his story.

Story by Andrew R McGhie

It was called the Wedderlea Hall(named for Wedderlea Farm near Lauder in the Borders, where my grandmother was born), and was situated on Graham Avenue. It was built in the mid-30s by my grandfather, Andrew Roxburgh McGhie, along with his two sons James Henderson, my father, and Andrew Roxburgh, my uncle. They were all builders. My father managed the dancing in the hall in the evenings. Apparently I was there in my pram going to sleep beside the band while they played the Platters' 'Street of Dreams'. The hall was destroyed by an incendiary bomb during the Blitz. When the sirens went off on the first night of the Blitz, all the dancers moved to the safety of the La Scala. I was not there that night as I was in Blawarthill Hospital with double pneumonia. I have a diagram of the hall my father drew for me 20 years, or so ago (see below).

My bedroom in Radnor Street overlooked the La Scala, and I went there frequently from an early age.

Picture 28: Local plan with Hall just visible

La Scala renovation 1960s

In the late 1960s the La Scala owners closed the building for renovation, including the demolition and lowering of the ironic landmark tower. Cinemas were facing increasingly tough times, against the new era of the television. Live music venues were also an alternative for customers.

The renovation converted the property into a dual-purpose cinema and bingo hall: claiming it was the first of its type in Scotland. Its doors were opened once more on 31 July 1969.

131

Big Skinny does a runner

Big Skinny started looking for a job once he turned sixteen, and soon a job came up at a chicken factory in Drumchapel called the Chicken Ranch. They were looking for a new security man. His friends told him to apply because he was quite tall, healthy and fit. So Big Skinny applied in person, and after a 2-minute interview (which consisted of, 'You'll do'), he got the job. The wages weren't great, but he was told that he could take a chicken home for his Christmas dinner, not just that year, but every Christmas Eve he worked there; that swayed it for him.

Big Skinny's job was to check the workers' bags when they were leaving the Chicken Ranch to make sure that no one took a dead chicken away with them. When he wasn't doing this, he had to fill bags full of feathers, which were then used to make pillows.

One day, a week before Christmas a new girl started at the Chicken Ranch. Her name was Gloria, she was skinny too, Big Skinny kinda fancied her, but then Big Skinny fancied any girl that blew a big bubble from her gum for him.

At the end of each evening, when it was time to stop work, the workers would come out in an orderly single file. Big Skinny would have to frisk the workers that looked suspicious. Big Skinny knew how to do this; he had seen it done so many times on TV. Clint Eastwood was his favourite film actor, and he loved the line, which

132

he had started to use when frisking the workers, 'Go ahead punk make my day.'

At the end of the working day on Christmas Eve, Big Skinny was excited. He knew he would get a free chicken to take home with him (it was in his contract) for his Christmas dinner once he had finished work. But, in the meantime, Big Skinny was checking out some bags, then, just like a flash of lighting, she whizzed past him. He could see the blonde curly hair and milky white thighs in a pair of shorts, and he just knew it was Gloria.

He left the Chicken Ranch and started after her. He could see that she had a chicken under each arm. He knew then that this was serious.

Big Skinny was fast, but Gloria could run like the wind. She was running fast, and he was hot in pursuit. They ran through Drumchapel, crossed the Boulevard motorway at the roundabout and into Drumry. They ran down the Drumry station stairway and into Linvale. They ran along the canal and into Clydebank Shopping Centre. There were shouts from people out for a walk or getting their messages. 'Are you out for a jog Big Skinny?'

'Naw,' was all Big Skinny could reply because he could hardly get his breath. He chased her into Dalmuir, and up the steep hill at Mountblow Road. He chased her across the Clydebank Golf Course, to the shouts of 'Stop chasing yer bird across the green Big Skinny.'

He chased her through the village of Duntocher, and up the windy road into Faifley. Big Skinny couldn't believe how bloody fit she was. 'She could run in the Olympics the next time they come around,' he thought. Eventually, Big Skinny realised that they had done a circuit and were nearly back at the Chicken Ranch in Drumchapel. But Gloria was getting further away from him, so he stopped running, and shouted 'Keep the chickens, and don't come back'.

When he got to the Chicken Ranch the gates were locked and all the lights of the factory were out, 'Aw naw,' he thought, 'I wiz tae get a chicken fur ma Christmas dinner.'

Just then the rain and snow started to come down. 'I don't believe it,' he shouted into the sky, 'now I'll need to make sandwiches fur ma Christmas dinner'… Poor Big Skinny, he had no luck.

Eyes down at the La Scala bingo hall

The great, La Scala managed to remain a cinema for another few years, but the increasing numbers of films being rented from video shops or shown on TV started the downward spiral and closure of many cinemas. The competition was too much for the La Scala and the cinema closed in 1983. However, it quickly reopened, this time as an EMI bingo hall, soon changing to Gala Bingo, which it remained until 2006.

But like the cinema, no amount of new owners or rebranding could change what people called the building, and it was still the La Scala. The bingo hall was a magnet for the new armies of bingo worshipers particularly with its good winning payouts. It had everything: you could sit and relax with a nice drink (alcoholic or otherwise) and after the bingo finished, you would be entertained by professional singers, comedians and entertainers.

This was a new era for the La Scala. The crowds were back, and they loved it.

Picture 29: Star Bingo and ABC Cinema advert

I remember when the bingo hall was packed every evening. I used to go with my mum when I was about 15 or 16. I enjoyed it, but I was embarrassed in case any of my mates would see me. It was worth the potential red face, though, because, you wouldn't believe it, I actually won on three separate occasions, a tenner a line. Don't laugh, because most of you will know that a tenner back then was a nice little bit of money. But I was getting to that stage where I was a little bit embarrassed sitting with my mum and her friends and stopped going. It wasn't long, though, before my younger sister was right in there, taking up my spot at the bingo next to my mum.

The following are some amusing stories, and I'm sure that many of you will have your own stories to tell.

One lady started work in the bingo hall, said:

> *I stayed in the cul-de-sac, which was only a short walk to the La Scala. I often walked along and went in to see who was about. I became the cleaning supervisor and worked there for seven or eight years. I wasn't a difficult boss, as we were all just a big happy lot, we had lots of laughs, and everyone done their work.*

Another story was from a man, who remembers, going with his mum on one occasion, but didn't win anything. He said she was never out of the bingo.

One man said:

> *I loved going to the bingo with my mum, and loved a hotdog. Years later I enjoyed meeting friends in the snooker club.*

Another man, who now lives in London said:

It was about 2005 when I went with my mum to the bingo, but I slept in and forgot to shout, 'FULL HOUSE', even though I had it. The next number came out and the woman next to us shouted. My mum wasn't too happy with me, and never spoke to me the whole way home.

Picture 30: Photo of the Star Bingo from The Clydebank Press

My four aunties worked as cleaners in the La Scala and used to go in to work at 5am every morning. They all got to their work on foot whether it was rain, hail or snow: two walked from Parkhall; one walked from Duntocher; and the other from Drumry.

My dad was in the La Scala the night of the Blitz.

The pregnant chair

Another story, that one woman recalled, was about the pregnant chair.

There was a particular chair in the staffroom of the Gala bingo dubbed 'The pregnant chair'. One woman loved that chair and would always sit on it during her breaks. When she became pregnant, the other members of staff joked about the chair making her pregnant. It was all a joke until, over the next couple of years, three other members of staff, who also enjoyed this comfortable chair, became pregnant. After the fifth member of staff became pregnant, no other female member of staff wanted to sit on it.

One guy who turned out to be a hero tells his story:

I went to work in the La Scala Bingo, before it was the Gala, it was the EMI. One night I done a rugby tackle to stop a thief escaping out the front door.

Another Clydebank lady tells her story, about her mum:

My mum was quite a reserved lady, a lady who had values, a high sense of self awareness, and upright in every way, in fact you could say that she was a pillar of strength within the community.

One evening a friend invited her to go for a game of bingo in the local chapel hall. There was nothing wrong with that, helping the church funds. But the next thing we knew, she was heading to the La Scala bingo Clydebank, as she had heard the prize money was better. Before we knew it, mum was off with her new friends to the County bingo in the Partick area of Glasgow where the prize money was seriously good. She had a great wee time to herself ... so much for the church funds!

One lady tells her story …

I worked, in the bingo hall, starting in the 1970s. There was a doorman who had worked at the La Scala for years, and told me so many stories. He remembered how badly the film The Exorcist *affected some people after watching it.*

He told me that the ghost (the Grey Lady) that many had seen, was seemingly a nurse during the war. The La Scala cinema was a makeshift mortuary during the Clydebank bombings. It was said that after she died, her ghostly spirit came back to the building.

Another lady recalls her story.

I remember as a kid, sneaking into the bingo hall, then going through some doors which led onto the emergency stairwell, from there you could open the emergency door. I would open it for some friends to get in. We would then climb the stairwell to the top of the cinema upstairs and get in free to see a film.

One evening after we sneaked in; we sat down to watch the film The Exorcist. *We were enjoying this horror film, eating sweets, sherbet, flying saucers, chocolate bars. Then all of a sudden the manager came over to us. We got out of our seats, and he started chasing us, we managed to get out the way we got in. Thinking back those were great memories.*

I sneaked into the La Scala, one time, to watch a film, and got caught. To make matters worse, the usherette that lived at the end of my street saw me. I did the walk of shame, which was so embarrassing. When I got older, I worked there as a bingo caller.

La Scala Bingo (my experiences)

Penny for the guy

A very funny story occurred one evening when my aunt, uncle and cousin, Joe, arrived from Glasgow to visit us. We were playing around the house, when I asked my cousin Joe Carr, if he had ever done penny for the guy. My Aunt Mary told us that he had tried a few places in Glasgow but had got nothing. So my mum asked me to help him and make a guy.

I couldn't find many things to make a guy, so … for a joke, I said, 'Why don't you become the guy?'

Living close to the dairy at the top of the hill, we managed to get a big empty cardboard egg box. We already had a false face from Halloween, so all we had to do was try it out.

I took him to the La Scala, front entrance, where the people were going into the bingo. I got him to lie in the box, with his feet and arms dangling out, and with his false face on, (I'm certain it was Dracula). He looked perfect, but I told him to keep very still. He did exactly that, and after we caught a lot of people going into the bingo, we decided that

143

we would wait for them coming back out. Sometimes Joe would move his head and add to the excitement and scare a few of the wee wives, but it was a fantastic success.

It was getting dark by the time my mum and aunt came down to the La Scala to get us up to the house, as my relatives were getting the last bus into Glasgow. When we got in and started to count the money and he had over £3 in loose change. Now let me tell you, that was a nice little whack of money for a night's work. The family were delighted for having visited us.

Now this kind of got me thinking, because, when I was doing penny for the guy, we normally used to stuff old clothes into a pair of trousers, and an old pillow inside a jacket, and a football for the head, and you would have to humph the bloody guy around everywhere, but this was much easier.

So the next year, I was the guy and sat in the box while my little sister asked for penny for the guy. I think because she was smaller, people never passed her by, and always gave her money. I'll tell you, we did make a few bob out of it, which (taking advice from our parents) we'd keep for our holidays.

Years later, my own children, Alison, Roger (Jnr) and Claire did the same. This time I sat across the road in my car so that I could keep a safety watch on them. They made a fortune and split it three ways.

How times have changed. In a funny way, perhaps, it made them streetwise at a young age, but they were still safe under my watchful eye, while I enjoyed the comfort of my car. The kids used the money for their holidays and were keen to continue this practice for a year or two more.

Clydebank celebrities

The following La Scala stories were sent to me by Bankies, who have done very well in their professions. From the hints that I give, see if you or your friends can work out who sent their stories to me.

Celebrity 1:

The first story is from a friend of mine who started a business after he left school. Well, that business just grew and grew. The next time you are going to buy a new kitchen, you just might go to one of his many showrooms. Here is his story:

> *Saturday morning was great at the ABC Morning Minors. Joining with hundreds of Bankies to watch* Flash Gordon, Lassie, *and God knows what else. We loved everything. Even occasionally opening the fire escape doors to allow some of your pals in free. Great times. Great fun, and all so memorable!*

146

Celebrity 2:

This person is very highly regarded in the community and is known for helping others. In fact, he took on a great project to open a centre in Clydebank to help people who have disabilities, people who are homeless, and people who are lonely. The centre has now become so very popular. This is his story:

The year was 1978. I was fifteen years old, and the anticipation was overwhelming. The musical, Grease, *was showing at the La Scala Clydebank. After school I rushed to the top of the hill and joined a queue like I'd never seen before. Black T-shirts and jeans everywhere. Some people, who came from wealthy families, had leather jackets on. Baseball boots were selling like hot cakes.*

What an experience. Every guy wanted to be Danny Zuko, and fancied Sandy.

I was so disappointed when the film had finished, so I lay down on the floor behind a row of seats, 'til the next showing (which seemed forever) and yes, I got to see it all over again. This time I was singing, as I had picked up some of the songs from the first show.

I would love those times back; they seemed more exciting.

Celebrity 3:

One of Clydebank's most famous son's has family and friends still here in Clydebank. He talks openly about his love for Clydebank, and part of his growing up. He tells his story of having a paper round:

When Singer's sewing machine factory would empty out, I'd be there to sell my papers, and I would hear the big foghorn on the River Clyde. I would be selling the Evening Times, *and if I could rush down Kilbowie Road, and get all the workers coming out of John Brown's shipyard, they would buy a paper from me, before they walked into a pub at the bottom of Kilbowie Road.*

There were a few pubs there. The Seven Seas Bar and the Borough Bar, I remember well. would position

148

myself well, and shout… 'Evening Times, Evening Times'. So they are the kind of memories that spring to mind.

And also going to the cinema hall in Clydebank (La Scala) where I saw loads of movies. I saw Star Wars and Live *and* Let Die. *I think the first movie I saw there was in the late 60s …* Bedknobs and Broomsticks. *It was a great movie.*

When I go back to Clydebank, I like to go to Dalmuir Park, where I have fond memories. There's a wee website, Call Yersel a Bankie, so I like to look at it now and then.

Celebrity 4:

Next we have a great Clydebank entertainer, who performs all over the UK and overseas.

My fondest memory of the La Scala, was when the film Rocky, *first came out. About twenty of us kids from Fullers Gate, Clydebank, all jogged down the hill to watch it. We all returned to see the film about four*

149

times. We loved acting like we were boxing training. Running up and down Kilbowie Road, which looking back now was a fair bit of training. It was mental, running in the pouring, pissin rain, and when we were getting drenched, snorters running. No one had much money; we were all quite poor in those days.

Also the matinees on a Sat morning ABC Minors, with the Littlest Hobo, as well as all the other great shows and characters. They were great memories.

I also did go to the Crucible Snooker Club in the La Scala many a time for a game of snooker.

I'm proud to say that I sang a song with this brilliant entertainer a few years back. I love one of his song's 'Maggie May' and his hairstyle.

Celebrity 5:

The next story that I'm going to tell, was conducted in a well-known Clydebank bar. It's called the Cleddans Bar. This enjoyable interview, over a few beers, was with a good friend who I've known for a considerable amount of years.

Perhaps you will know, who, and what, this is about as the story unfolds.

This person played in a Clydebank band! The band was formed in about 1977 and broke up in the early 1980s. There were five members of the band. They played at different venues in Clydebank: La Scala cinema, the Hub Community Centre, Edinbarnet School, the Peel Pub, Drumchapel, and other venues further afield.

One incident is that the manager of the band got a phone call on a Friday evening in 1978 to see if the band could perform, at short notice, the next day at the ABC Morning Minors. This was agreed and the band played Slade numbers (you *must* remember Slade) for an hour and a half. It turned out to be a brilliant performance and was very successful, with the band gaining recognition. From this point on, a massive amount of locals started to follow the band.

Unfortunately there was one gig that became memorable for the wrong reasons. You may well remember it. It was the 1978/79 firework display at Clydebank High Park. A high platform was built for the performance of this thriving

151

young band and over a thousand locals turned up to listen to them. But sometimes nature can strike a cruel blow (especially in Scotland), and due to heavy rainfall, coupled with electrical problems, the performance had to be cancelled,.

I seemed to be always in the thick of things in Clydebank, because as a teenager I used to go to the Hub Community Hall on a Saturday evening, and the place would be packed. Now, thinking back, I didn't realise when I was watching and listening to this local band all those years ago that they would be included in part of the La Scala's great history.

   a) What was the name of the band?

   b) Who did I interview?

   c) Who were the other four band members?

Celebrity 6:

Now my next celebrity, is well known around Clydebank, you will see that he gives his story in quite clear detail.

I don't have many memories of the La Scala growing up in the 50s. I lived in Yoker, right on the boundary of

Clydebank, and not having a lot of money as children, we had to walk most places, so the La Scala would have been a long walk. My two sisters and I ran about together everywhere, and our cinemas were the Empire, and the Bank on Glasgow Road. That was until the Empire burned down, and then it was the Bank cinema every week.

The only memory we have of the La Scala was going to see Jason and the Argonauts *in the 1960s. I went with my two sisters. I can remember that I was worried that we were going to be late, and we walked-ran and all the way. It was a ground-breaking movie at the time because of Ray Harryhausen's special effects. A brilliant movie for us kids.*

I got married in 1974 and started keeping a diary. As an adult, it was Glasgow town for the movies as my wife, before we got married, worked in the town. I would meet her coming out of work and we would usually go to the Wimpy then the cinema.

In my diary I visited the La Scala a few times, which was called the ABC Clydebank by then.

These are the extracts from my diary:

4 April 1975 Friday: Helen and I went up to the ABC Clydebank to see *Airport 75* about a jumbo jet that gets hit by a small plane and kills the crew. Very tense.

18 April 1975 Friday: Helen and I went up to the ABC Clydebank. We are getting lazy and got a taxi up. We saw *Eskimo Nell* and *The Visitor*.

3 May 1975 Saturday: Helen and I went up to the ABC Clydebank and saw *Hex* and *Dirty Mary, Crazy Larry*.

26 November 1975 Wednesday: Helen and I went up to the ABC Clydebank to see *The Klansman* starring Lee Marvin and Richard Burton. It was a very good tense drama with a couple of funny bits thrown in.

15 October 1976 Friday: Helen asked us if we wanted to go to the pictures. She ran us up in the car. We saw *Jaws*. A terrific picture about a shark that terrorises a holiday resort.

7 December 1976 Tuesday: We went to the ABC Clydebank and saw *Squirm* about worms that attack humans. It was horrible.

5 January 1977 Wednesday: Helen and I went to the ABC Clydebank Cinema. We saw an Elvis film called *Charro*, a cowboy film and then *Future World*, a follow-up to *Westworld*. It was about a holiday camp full of robots, and people went there for fun and adventure.

1 April 1977 Friday: Helen and I went up to the ABC Clydebank and saw *The Omen*, a black magic film. It was not bad. Some of it was boring, but some of it was quite good.

25 May 1977 Wednesday: We went up to Faifley and collected Paul and we went to the pictures and saw *Carrie*. It was supposed to be horrific, but it wasn't as bad as was made out. The picture on with it, *Gator*, was very good.

10 June 1977 Friday: We went up to the ABC Clydebank and saw *The Sentinel* a horror picture about devils. *The Midnight Man* was also on with it. It was a good film also.

27 July 1977 Wednesday: We went round to collect Anne and went up to the ABC Clydebank to see *Sinbad and the Eye of the Tiger*. It was not a very good picture. The picture *Benji*, which was on with it, was better, but not much.

By 1977 Helen was expecting our first child. We were moving house and getting ready for the baby arriving.

I also took up 35mm photography. Cinema took a back seat from then on.

In 1981 the family and I built a hut from scratch up at Carbeth and we spent most weekends and holidays up there.

Answers to Celebrity Quiz:

1. Jim McCay (owner of Kitchen Depot)

2. Jim McLaren (Golden Friendships Club)

3. Marti Pellow (Wet, Wet, Wet singer and entertainer)

4. James Frew (Rod Stewart tribute act)

5.

    a) The band was called STRACY

    b) Gary McLaren

    c) Martin Preson, Billie Massie, Tam McManus
    and Tazz Gallagher

6. Owen McGuigan (Clydebank historian)

Picture 32: Stracy (l-r) Martin Preston, Billy Massie, Tam McManus, Tazz Gallagher, Gary James McLaren

The Crucible Snooker Club

The Crucible Snooker Club, opened to the public in 1984 and became very popular with the new, younger generation who enjoyed watching snooker on TV. Snooker clubs, with modern leisure facilities, were springing up all over the UK. There was nothing better than meeting up with your friends at the La Scala Crucible. You could have a substantial snack with a beer or two, at great prices. And let's not forget the Crucible Karaoke. Here's a mixture of stories about the snooker room and the karaoke singers down at the bar.

> Some days, at the weekend, it was so busy that you had to put your name on the list and wait in the queue. The place had fourteen full-size snooker tables. There were two private rooms, and two pool tables. The beer was good, and the waitresses were tasty too. If you got papped out of the tournament, you would head down to the karaoke. What a place.
>
> I loved the La Scala Clydebank, in fact I got a job in the Crucible Snooker Club, working in the reception. In those days, I had a fantastic figure, and often got told I

was good looking, maybe I should have been a model. I was never stuck for a boyfriend; all the guys fancied me. I think that I helped to increase the membership, when I worked there, and the place was often busy.

Happy Memories ...

Another story of working in the bar for a short period of time.

I was young but got a job in the Crucible Snooker Club. In those days I was a bit shy, and quite modest, but the clients, mostly guys were great, the banter and gossip were brilliant. I enjoyed the experience, and it stuck by me in other jobs in the future. Great memories ...

The Singer ....

I was a regular at the Crucible Snooker Club where, at the weekend, there was karaoke. Instead of my dreams of being a great snooker player, I found out that I had a talent for singing. It was at the Crucible that I began on the road and took off with my singing career.

The lover ….

I went to the Crucible because I fancied the girl that worked at the reception. I can't remember her name, but she was lovely. All the guys fancied her.

Competition …

I loved my snooker nights at the La Scala Crucible, especially at the Sunday night handicap snooker tournament. The night would be polished off with some good old karaoke in the bar. You could drink quite late on a Sunday night, but then came the Monday morning hangovers. Those were the days.

The champions …

David Skewis (Snr) and David Skewis (Jnr) won the father and son club championship there in 1986/87. The trophy was presented by Mandy Fisher who was the woman's world snooker champion in 1984. David (Jnr) met his wife there as she worked in the bingo downstairs. They celebrate 30 years married in 2022.

Picture 33: David Skewis (Snr) and David Skewis (Jnr) winning Crucible snooker championship (c.1986)

La Scala happy and sad times

There were some sad memories at the La Scala ABC Morning Minors …

One particular story was about a boy, but more probably a man, who went to the Morning Minors every Saturday morning. This young man had Down syndrome.

Everyone knew him and knew that he used to sit in the same seat every week. If anyone else went near the seat, others would say, 'You can't sit there, that's daft Donald's seat.'

161

The children were not being disrespectful, it's just that in those days the children thought that you were silly or daft if you were not like them. Nowadays children are so much aware of others' disabilities, and don't say things that would hurt feelings.

Anyway, Donald loved all the movies, cartoons and films, and all that was going around him at the ABC Minors. At the end of the morning screening, he would stand for the national anthem, as hordes of screaming kids would stampede towards the exit doors. Donald wouldn't walk along the pavement, but would ride an imaginary horse, and gallop along the road. Sadly, one day he got knocked down, and later died in hospital.

His name was Donald Rose.

Great White Angel shouldn't have been destroyed

During the making of this book, I spoke to some patriotic Bankies, and most came to the same conclusion, that the La Scala should have not been completely destroyed.

Some stated that they should have kept the facia (the front of

162

the building), in remembrance, just like the bingo halls and old cinemas in Anniesland and Muirend, Glasgow, where flats were built behind the facia.

But the death sentence was announced, and the bulldozers moved in.

I personally think that the La Scala picture house should have been kept in defiance of the German Luftwaffe bombers. When you think of it, what a great gesture it would have been to leave a memorial to the brave men and women who suffered during those two nights of hell.

In fairness to the authorities, when they did take the La Scala down, it was riddled with asbestos. The building was so bad that a special workforce had to be employed for months after the destruction of this great magnificent building, to get rid of the huge amount of asbestos. Perhaps we didn't want that health hazard in our Clydebank town.

Picture 34: La Scala becomes a 'development opportunity'

Picture 35: The sad demise of La Scala

Picture 36: Preparation for demolition

Picture 37: Ready for Demolition

165

Picture 38:Start of demolition - view from Second Avenue

Picture 39: Demolition under way

I'm sure we will all agree that it was not only a landmark, but at the very heart of Clydebank and, like Singer's clock and other landmarks, we should not have taken away the visual history of Clydebank.

166

What happened to Big Skinny?

Now most of you will be wondering as you come to the end of the book, what exactly happened to Big Skinny, that went to the La Scala cinema and couldnae find a seat, because Big Skinny had quite a history with the La Scala.

Big Skinny sometimes went out on a Friday or Saturday night, sometimes even both nights, looking for a bird. One evening, during lights up at the break, he got chatting to this lovely usherette who was selling ice cream down in front of the big screen. Her name was Julie Ann, blond and very good looking. They started dating and before long, they were married, and within the first five years they had four children. Big Skinny wasn't slow, but things didn't quite work out and eventually Julie Ann left him for a travelling ice cream salesman.

As you can imagine, Big Skinny was devastated when she packed up and took the four children with her. She did leave him the dog, which Big Skinny wasn't too happy about as the dog didn't like him too much and kept biting his leg.

Not long after the divorce Big Skinny wanted to start dating and before long, he was back at his old hunting ground at the La Scala, looking again for a bird. One evening, just as he after he bought his choc ice and KP peanuts, he hurried back to his seat, and bumped into a lovely girl. She was dark-haired and had a lovely smile. She apologised for bumping into him and the mess that his suit was

168

in. Big Skinny wasn't caring about the mess, or his bloody suit, he was more interested in this dark-haired beauty. She was there on her own, so he invited her back to his row where there was an empty seat next to his. She was a bit of a chatterbox, and she told Big Skinny that she worked in schools helping underprivileged kids.

She asked what he worked at. He told her that he worked in a chocolate factory making new chocolate bars called Chocolate Mackaracas. The machines that he worked on were always breaking down and he was so good at fixing them that the management told him that he should think about furthering his career as an engineer.

At this stage in his life Big Skinny, who had a good business brain, decided to try different opportunities to making a living. Unfortunately, Big Skinny and Carol Ann weren't that well suited, and eventually split up. A new janitor started work at her school, and after a whirlwind romance, she married him.

Then out of the blue, a little blonde turned up one evening near Christmas. She was smartly dressed, with a rich smell of continental perfume. She turned heads as she walked up the aisle of the cinema. The cinema was showing a romantic film, *Endless Love*, that night and well, Big Skinny was a real romantic at heart, wasn't he? But he wasn't lucky in love, in fact he could pick his nose better than picking a bird. Undeterred, Big Skinny got talking to her, and she was more than a match for him with her quick one-liners.

She reminded Big Skinny of a good-looking gremlin, you know, the kind that has lush pink lipstick, and beautiful bright green flashing eyes. He knew he wanted to cuddle her, but it was a bit too soon to make his move. Big Skinny started dating her and called her 'Baby', which she liked.

Was this a match? Certainly they couldn't keep their hands off one another. Saturday nights were no longer La Scala cinema nights, instead it was off to Glasgow for boogie nights, and they both danced the night away.

Alas, shortly after, the romance came to an end, and Big Skinny and Baby broke up. Baby went on to meet a managing director of a toy store, and Big Skinny had to start looking again. (Incidentally Big Skinny and Baby remained friends through the years.)

One summery evening, a tall, leggy good-looking woman came into the cinema with her pal. It was a sad romantic movie, *Remember Me,* that was on, and Big Skinny sat there munching on his popcorn with tears in his eyes. He couldn't quite understand why these two girls in the seats in front of him were giggling and laughing when the film was so sad. Big Skinny tapped on the tallest girl's shoulder to tell them to keep down the laughing, and like a bolt from the blue, their eyes meet. WOW! Now this could be it; instant attraction.

170

When the lights went up, Big Skinny asked the girls were they came from. They told him that they were local, but Big Skinny, who knew everyone, and everyone knew Big Skinny, knew that these two dolls were new on the block.

The taller of the two girls introduced herself as Maureen and he told them that he was Jim Slim, but everyone called him Big Skinny. A date was put on for a meet up the following week. The date worked very well, a whirlwind romance followed, and holidays in the sun were on the menu. Marriage followed with one, two, three children, made to order, and more planned for the future.

Big Skinny was so happy. His new wife had a good job, and Big Skinny decided to go back into education. Before long, he had gained top certificates in different fields of expertise in Marine Engineering. Big Skinny was learning fast and began to make huge strides in the world of business.

But sometimes in life things just don't turn out the way you want them, and as the years dwindled by, Big Skinny didn't see what was coming. First there was a separation, then a divorce.

An old era was coming to an end. The La Scala building closed down, never to reopen. There were no more Friday or Saturday nights or any nights for that matter, that Big Skinny could wander the aisles looking for a bird.

He never did marry again but is always on the lookout for a date. I got to know this guy quite well. He still wanders around Clydebank. Perhaps the next time that you are out and about in Clydebank, and you see a charismatic chap with a smile, stopping to talk to everyone he meets, it just could be Big Skinny that you're looking at …

La Scala Quiz

What was happening in 1938?

1. Which monarch was on the throne?
2. Which Scottish team won the Scottish (Football) Cup?
3. What zoo opened in London?
4. How much was a loaf of bread?
5. What was the average cost of a car?
6. How much would a terraced house cost?
7. What was the average yearly wage?
8. What would £100 in 1938 be worth in 2022?
9. What was the very first film shown at the Clydebank La Scala?

The beginning and end of an era

1. When did the Clydebank Blitz happen?
2. When did the La Scala, Clydebank officially open? Why was it a special date?
3. What year did the La Scala go on sale by public auction, and what was the asking price?

4. A woman was queuing to get into the bingo. Who was in the hearse she put a flower on?

5. Where was the great La Scala cinema situated in Clydebank?

6. What was that area known as?

7. Can you give a brief description of what the La Scala looked like from the outside?

8. The La Scala closed in 1941: why and for how long?

9. Who took over the La Scala in 1959?

10. What year did the La Scala Clydebank close for the last time?

11. What year was smoking banned in public places?

12. Why do you think that smoking was banned in public places?

13. In 2016, the Clydebank Housing Association announced a merger to build new houses on the site. What was the name of the company that would build the houses?

A piece of nostalgia / Setting the scene

1. Name three items you could buy from the kiosk or usherette.

2. Why do you think that going to the cinema in those days was a good thing to do?

3. How did Clydebank get its name?

4. By 1885, Clydebank town was home to the largest factory in the world. What was its name? How many workers were employed there in 1913?
5. The author took up Shipbuilding Engineering shortly after school. What company did he work for and who had ordered the ships?
6. What was his trade?

Clydebank Blitz / Clydebank after the Blitz

1. What two nights did the German bombers bomb Clydebank?
2. The German bombers planned to bomb John Brown Shipbuilders; did they succeed?
3. What did the Bankies do to divert most of the German bombs?
4. What was the film showing at the La Scala on the first night of the Blitz?
5. Why do you think the La Scala cinema was called a 'Huge White Guardian Angel'?
6. When someone's granny got blown into the Clydebank Canal, who fished her out?
7. A mother looked up at the billboard and the film showing was called *Gone with the Wind*. What did she say?
8. What did the La Scala store in the cinema just after the war?
9. Why was a lot of the furniture not reclaimed?

10. Where was the unclaimed furniture eventually taken to?
11. What was 'the destroyer'?

La Scala Cinema

1. How old was Roger when he had his first experience of going to the cinema?
2. Who took him?
3. Why couldn't his dad watch him?
4. Why did he look taller going into the cinema?
5. Did he enjoy the film?
6. His mother and aunt tried the same procedure another time, was it successful again?
7. Years later, this procedure would be repeated to get his youngest daughter, Claire, into the new Empire Cinema in the Clydebank Shopping Centre. What were they trying to see?
8. When the author was little he played football outside the La Scala cinema. Which member of his family did the same thing, years later?
9. When out looking for his daughter Alison, the author heard her voice which frightened him. Why?
10. Name three things that some people took with them to eat at the La Scala?
11. One guy had to have a few beers before going to the La Scala. Why?

12. Why did one guy, who loved a drink, never get drunk when he went to the La Scala?

13. What happened when about a dozen friends got drunk on Old England at the La Scala?

14. What was a popular wine drink in those days? (An advert for it appears in the book).

Big Skinny and the bogey

1. What was the craze around Clydebank in those days?
2. What was a bogey?
3. What did Big Skinny forget to put on his bogey?
4. When Big Skinny crashed into the bins, what damage did he do?

Was it haunted?

1. Who was the ghost who haunted the La Scala, Clydebank?
2. What was the story about the Lady-in-Grey?
3. What other use did the La Scala have during the war?

Battle on the Hill

1. What year did the Battle on the Hill take place?
2. What was the name of the film showing that evening?
3. Who were the two gangs involved in the fight?
4. One girl took off her high heels and ran through the cinema. How did she get out?

5. When the doorman said, 'You can leave the easy way or leave the hard way', what did he mean?

Crying on a date / La Scala Cinema curtains / Dates, romance and love

1. Name one film that had someone crying on a date.
2. Give a brief description of the elegant curtains that the La Scala had in its early years?
3. Why did one brother take his sister to all the Doris Day movies?
4. Why was a guy who waited on his date outside the La Scala, broken hearted?
5. One woman met her future husband at the La Scala. How long have they been married?
6. Why did one girl say her date was ruined when she went to see a James Bond film?
7. One girl went on a date to see *My Fair Lady* but realised that her date wasn't the one for her. What did she do?
8. One lady's boyfriend told her to take a drag of his cigarette. What happened when she did?

Big Skinny's train journey

1. Where was Big Skinny waiting for the train? What train station was he going to?
2. Why didn't Big Skinny get off at Queens Street?
3. Where did Big Skinny eventually get off?

4. How much money did Big Skinny have to get him home?
5. How did Big Skinny get home? How long did it take him?

La Scala poems / La Scala stories

1. Who wrote 'Apricot-coloured Duchess?'
2. Who wrote 'A Theatre of Dreams'?
3. Who wrote 'The Clydebank ABC?', 'A Hard Day's Night' (about the legendary gang fight at the La Scala) and King Kong Escapes Clydebank ABC 1968'?
4. Who wrote 'La Scala on the Hill'?
5. Who wrote 'A Pocket Full of Pennies'?
6. Who wrote 'The Thrill at the Tap a ra Hill'?
7. Who wrote 'When I Was Young'?
8. Who wrote 'Saturday Night at the Movies'?

Heydays! La Scala films and memories

1. If you queued to the right-hand side of the La Scala, where would it take you?
2. If you queued to the left-hand side, where would it take you?
3. What month and year is the La Scala Programme for?
4. What was one of the last films to be shown at the La Scala cinema?
5. What was the first cinemascope in the La Scala?

178

6. One girl broke her heart at the end of the film *ET*. Why?

Saturday Morning Minors

1. Why could Roger not sleep well on a Friday night?
2. What did Roger and other kids do with the lolly sticks they collected from the floor?
3. What instructions did Roger give his 5-year-old little sister?
4. Why did parents like their kids to go to the Morning Minors on a Saturday?
5. When Roger's father had a wee win on the horses on Saturday, what might happen on Sunday?
6. What TV programme would frighten the life out of Roger (and who in particular)?
7. When the author lived at 7 Crown Avenue, what was the street known as?
8. How much was admission to the Saturday Morning Minors?
9. Who normally took the wee ones on a Saturday morning to the ABC Minors?
10. What were the typical clothes worn in those days?
11. Can you remember the ABC Minors Song?
12. Roger won first prize at the Morning Minors Halloween party; what was he dressed as?
13. Can you describe how his mum made the costume?
14. What did he win?

15. Why did Roger's little sister win a big box of chocolates?

16. Who won the singing contest, by singing the Morning Minors' song (with bit of action)?

17. What happened if you took a birthday card with you to the ABC Morning Minors? What would they get you to do?

18. When the good guys were beating the bad guys, what did everyone shout?

19. Why did the cinema attendants sometimes find it difficult dealing with the kids?

20. Can you name some of the Disney cartoons that they showed?

21. Which films can you remember that were shown? What did you like? What did you not like?

22. When a guy had his motorcycle stolen twice outside the La Scala, where did he find it?

Big Skinny gets well and truly tanned

1. When Big Skinny looked out of his window, what did he see?

2. When Big Skinny decided to go sunbathing, what did he forget to pack?

3. When someone from Goldenhill shouted, 'Where you going today?' What did he shout back?

4. Which park did Big Skinny go to?

5. Where did Big Skinny find a place to sunbathe?

6. What part of Big Skinny was not burnt?

Memorable movies

1. What very memorable film hit the La Scala in 1977?
2. Why was it so different to other films?
3. What did the audience wear when they went to see *Grease*?
4. What did the *Grease* audience do during the interval?
5. Who starred in *Grease*?

The local area

1. What were the two well-known shops on Radnor Street called?
2. What was the pub called at the corner of Radnor Street and Kilbowie Road? (It's still there.)
3. Why did Roger's father send him to get razor blades for shaving on a Saturday night?
4. Where did he go to buy them?
5. Where did Roger and lots of other kids buy their sweets from?
6. What was the name of the chippy on Radnor Street?
7. What might you get if you took newspapers into the chippy?
8. What sometimes happened while you waited for your chips or supper?
9. Why did Roger sometimes run up Kilbowie Road after coming out of the La Scala?

181

10. What did Roger's father take home with him on a Saturday night?
11. What was rigged out as a vet outside the La Scala in the 50s & 60s?
12. Where was the Wedderlea Dance Hall situated?
13. On the first night of the Blitz, where did the dancers from the dance hall run to for safety?
14. Why, in the late 60s, did the La Scala cinema close for a short period of time?
15. What did the La Scala claim to have after the renovation?

Big Skinny does a runner

1. Where did Big Skinny get his first job?
2. What were the perks of the job?
3. What was the name of the girl who started work at the chicken factory?
4. What did she run out of the factory with?
5. Name three areas where Big Skinny chased her?
6. Was she a fast runner?
7. Why do you think Big Skinny only had a sandwich for his Christmas dinner?

Eyes down at the La Scala Bingo Hall

1. In 1983, the EMI Bingo closed. What was it renamed as?
2. What year did the Gala Bingo close?

3. Why did so many people go to the bingo?
4. One person said his mother wouldn't speak to him after the bingo one night. Why?
5. How did the Pregnant Chair get its name?
6. What did one of the doormen do to stop a thief getting out of the La Scala Bingo Hall?
7. What did the author do to make the Guy in the box look more realistic?
8. Why do you think, in those days, people were more astute and streetwise?

Celebrities

1. Who was the Clydebank man who founded the Kitchen Depot and loved the ABC Minors?
2. Who is highly regarded in Clydebank Golden Friendships Club? He went to see *Grease* in 1978.
3. Who is the international star who sold the *Evening Times* in Clydebank. He loved watching *Star Wars* in the La Scala.
4. Who is the fantastic (Rod Stewart) entertainer who loved the film *Rocky* and used to jog up and down Kilbowie Road?
5. Who played with the band Stracy at the La Scala, Clydebank?
6. Who is the Clydebank historian? He went with his wife, Helen, to see *Jaws* in 1976.

The Crucible Snooker Club

1. What year was the Crucible Snooker Club opened?
2. Why was playing snooker becoming so popular?
3. What extra entertainment did they have at the snooker club?
4. What did one guy do when he found out he had a talent for singing?
5. Who were the father and son who won the club championship in 1986/87?
6. One guy went to the Crucible Club for a reason other than snooker. What was it?

La Scala happy times sad times / Great White Angel

1. Who was the guy who had Down Syndrome and loved the Saturday ABC Morning Minors?
2. What happened to him?
3. Why do you think the La Scala cinema shouldn't have been knocked down?
4. What do you think Roger felt about keeping the La Scala?

What happened to Big Skinny?

1. Where was Big Skinny's ideal place looking for a date?
2. What was the name of Big Skinny's first love?
3. Who did she leave Big Skinny for?

4. What was the name of the chocolate bars that Big Skinny said he made at the chocolate factory?

5. His new dark-haired beautiful girlfriend, Carol Ann, worked in schools. What was her job?

6. Who did Carol Ann leave Big Skinny for?

7. His next bird was a wee blonde-haired woman. What would Big Skinny call her?

8. What did she remind Big Skinny of?

9. Who did she run off with?

10. Who kept laughing during the film at the La Scala?

11. What did Big Skinny say his name was?

12. After a whirlwind romance, how many children did they have?

13. Apart from Engineering what did Big Skinny do well in?

14. Where might you see Big Skinny if you're out shopping?

Answers

What Was Happening in 1938?

1. George VI.
2. East Fife ... O yes they did!
3. London Children Zoo.
4. Tuppence (old money).
5. £170.
6. £600 – £750.
7. Approx. £165.
8. £7000.
9. *Maytime Music*.

The beginning and end of an era

1. 13–15 March 1941.
2. 14 February 1938 (St Valentine's Day).
3. 2013. Asking price £100,000.
4. Her husband.
5. Halfway up Kilbowie Road, on Graham Avenue.
6. The Holy City.
7. Beautiful deco design. Cream-coloured high columns. The tower stood tall with neon lighting.
8. It closed because of the war. It remained closed for three years and reopened in 1944.
9. Associated British Cinemas (ABC).
10. 19 February 1983.
11. 2006.

12. Negative effects of passive smoking were recognised e.g. lung disease, heart disease, cancer.
13. A.S. Homes (Scotland) Ltd.

A piece of nostalgia / Setting the scene

1. Kiora Orange Juice, Smiths Crisps, KP Peanuts.
2. Not everyone had TVs. People got the news from *Pathe News*. You could also make friends or start relationships.
3. As shipbuilding took off along the River Clyde more land was needed. Ships started being built further down the river from Govan. The area become industrialised, resulting in a police station being built, but a name was needed. Banks of the Clyde, hence: Clydebank.
4. Singer's Sewing Machine factory employed 14,000 workers by 1913.
5. Yarrow Shipbuilders. The Royal Navy.
6. Trade Engineer.

Clydebank Blitz / Clydebank after the Blitz

1. The nights of 13 and 14 March 1941.
2. No.
3. They put lights along the Boulevard Road, which is now part of the motorway.
4. It was a Shirley Temple film.

5. Because it saved the lives of those who remained inside the building.
6. Their grandpa.
7. 'Aye, it's gone with the wind all right!'
8. The cinema was crammed with furniture from bombed-out houses.
9. Some of the people had died, and some just moved away.
10. The Council in Barnes Street, Clydebank.
11. It was a machine that broke up the unclaimed furniture.

La Scala Cinema

1. Just started primary school, he was about 5-years old.
2. His mum and aunt.
3. His dad was working overtime, to help pay the bills.
4. The two women lifted him up to make him look taller.
5. No. He fell asleep halfway through it.
6. No. They had to go home.
7. Her mum and big sister dressed her up and put make-up on her, and for good measure, a bra. She was told to just keep smiling, though she was scary looking, and was walked in, with feet off the ground. She also fell asleep.

8. His son, Roger (Jnr).

9. She had climbed through the high turrets at the main front entrance, about 20-foot high.

10. Sandwiches, a kebab or a fish supper.

11. To pick up courage to look for the perfect woman.

12. In case he got a lumber (a date).

13. They laughed at all the sad parts in the film.

14. Eldorado wine. Known as the L D.

Big Skinny and the bogey

1. The bogey.

2. A cart made of a small plank of wood (about 3-foot), attached to an old set of pram wheels.

3. Brakes.

4. Concussion, and no toe nails.

Was it haunted?

1. The Lady-in-Grey or the Grey Lady.

2. She was said to be looking for her daughter who was buried under the La Scala.

3. It was used as a temporary mortuary.

Battle on the Hill

1. 1965.

2. *Help!* starring The Beatles.

3. Clydebank boys and the Drumchapel boys (known as The Drum).

4. The exit door.
5. 'You can walk out the front door or get thrown through it.'

Crying on a date / La Scala Cinema curtains / Dates, romance and love

1. *Last Snows of Spring* or *Ring of Bright Water*.
2. One had the print of the *Queen Mary*, the other had New York skyscrapers on it. When the curtains were closed, it gave the illusion of sailing to New York.
3. Because he was in love with Doris Day.
4. She never turned up.
5. 50 years.
6. When she turned around to see who was behind her, she saw her two brothers.
7. She said she was going to the toilet and hopped it out the front door.
8. She got dizzy and fell down the stairs.

Big Skinny's train journey

1. He was waiting at Dalmuir and going to Singer's Station.
2. The lock on the toilet door jammed.
3. Waverly Station, Edinburgh.
4. The price of a packet of crisps.
5. He walked. Two days.

La Scala poems / La Scala stories

1. Lesley Jane Lang
2. Martin Hopkins
3. Hamish Mac Donald
4. Boyd McNicol
5. Larry, Curly and Moe
6. Wolfman Bernie Logue
7. Alex Doherty
8. Boyd McNicol

Heydays! La Scala films and memories

1. The Stalls.
2. The Balcony.
3. September 1949.
4. *ET.*
5. *The Robe.*
6. Because he went home.

Saturday Morning Minors

1. Because Saturday was Morning Minors ABC day. Singing, laughing and games.
2. To weave and make them into boomerangs to fire around the cinema.
3. To look for any lolly sticks that she could find, so that he could make boomerangs to fire.
4. So that shopping, washing school uniforms, and general tidying up could be done.

5. A trip down the water to Rothsay, with fish suppers on the beach for the family.
6. *Doctor Who* (the Daleks).
7. 'Top of the Hill'.
8. Sixpence (old money).
9. Big brothers, or sisters, or cousins, or friends.
10. Coat fastened with waist belt, or warm tunic, with a balaclava to keep your head warm.
11. Sing it or learn it and sing it.
12. A very old man.
13. She cut up old trousers, shortened them and put braces on, gave him a collarless grandpa shirt. Then, she fixed an old white handkerchief around his face, cutting out pieces for eyes, nose and mouth, and lined with a dark pencil. She made a wig (out of her hair buns) bushy eyebrows and moustache, which were glued onto the handkerchief face. It was fantastic.
14. A big tin of Quality Street.
15. She won the Easter bonnet contest, thanks again to the artistic talents of their mum.
16. The author, 'Ol Blue Eyes' himself.
17. You would get in for nothing. You were put up on the stage, and everyone sang 'Happy Birthday' to you, and you got sweets. Some kids had three birthdays or more in a year!
18. 'Easy – Easy – Easy!'

19. They were always running around until the films came on.
20. Bugs Bunny, Popeye, Looney Tunes.
21. Discuss.
22. Drumchapel.

Big Skinny gets well and truly tanned

1. Two cows having a good munch on Mrs Murphy's bedsheets.
2. Suntan lotion.
3. 'I'm going to get suntanned'.
4. Dalmuir Park, Clydebank.
5. On the island for ducks and swans.
6. His big white eyes.

Memorable movies

1. *Star Wars*.
2. Special effects with new technology and out-of-this-world ideas.
3. They were all dressed up in their *Grease* outfits.
4. They got up on stage or danced in the passageways.
5. John Travolta and Olivia Newton John.

The local area

1. Billy Bellingham's Newsagents and McNaughtan's Chippy.
2. The Cleddans Bar.

3. Because he was getting spruced up for going out for a drink.
4. Billy Bellingham's Newsagent.
5. Billy Bellingham's Newsagent.
6. McNaughtan's Chippy.
7. Lots of extra chips.
8. A fight would break out amongst the local lads.
9. To get a bag of chips before closing time.
10. A fish supper and a bottle of orange.
11. A three-tonne army truck.
12. Across from the La Scala (corner of Graham Avenue and Kilbowie Road). See Picture 22.
13. The La Scala.
14. Renovation work (demolition and lowering of the ironic landmark tower).
15. The first dual-purpose cinema and bingo hall.

Big Skinny does a runner

1. In a chicken factory in Drumchapel.
2. A free chicken on Christmas Eve.
3. Gloria.
4. Two chickens, one under each arm.
5. Drumry Train Station, Clydebank Shopping Centre, Dalmuir.
6. Yes she was, she could run faster than Big Skinny.
7. Think about it?

Eyes down at the La Scala Bingo Hall

1. Gala Bingo.
2. 2006.
3. Nice surroundings, good entertainment, having a drink and good prizes.
4. He slept in and didn't shout for a full house.
5. Many women who sat on it got pregnant.
6. A diving rugby tackle to take him down.
7. He dressed up and sat in the box himself, moving his head very slowly, to the amusement of the people. His children collected the money.
8. They knew exactly what was going on around and about them. The older generation were very clever and taught their own kids the way of the world.

Celebrities

1. Jim McCay
2. Jim McLaren
3. Marti Pellow
4. James Frew
5. Gary McLaren
6. Owen McGuigan

The Crucible Snooker Club

1. 1984.
2. The younger generation liked it, and snooker clubs were the new craze.

3. Karaoke.
4. He became a professional singer.
5. David Skewis (Snr) & David Skewis (Jnr).
6. Because he was in love with a girl who worked there and wanted to see her.

La Scala happy times sad times / Great White Angel

1. Donald Rose.
2. Sadly he had a tragic accident. He was knocked down.
3. Open for debate.
4. He felt that the La Scala may have been kept in defiance of the German bombers who failed to destroy this iconic building. In fairness to the authorities, the building was riddled with asbestos and could have caused major health concerns. Still the front columns and beautiful décor at the front could have been preserved as a memory for the Bankies.

What happened to Big Skinny?

1. The La Scala cinema.
2. Julie Ann.
3. A travelling ice cream salesman.
4. Mackaracas.
5. She helped underprivileged kids.
6. A new janny who started at the school.
7. Baby.

8. A good-looking gremlin … Green flashing eyes and blood red lipstick.
9. The Managing Director of a toy store.
10. Maureen.
11. Slim Jim, but everyone calls him Big Skinny.
12. Three.
13. Business.
14. Wandering around Clydebank talking to everyone.

Note From the Author:

Perhaps you can make up your own quiz. There are so many stories in this book to pick from. You could pick teams to test each other's knowledge once you've read the book or you could write stories inspired by some of the characters. Perhaps you could compare your memories with those of your friends or of the people in the book. Once you've read this book you might want to read it again to check your answers.

All proceeds from this book will be donated to charity.

La Scala programme Sept 1949

Courtesy of Christine Pert

LA SCALA

CLYDEBANK'S SUPER CINEMA

Telephone: CLYDEBANK 1279.

Manager: ANGUS MACNAB

PROGRAMME

FOR
SEPTEMBER, 1949

2

— LA SCALA - CLYDEBANK —

SEPTEMBER ATTRACTIONS AT A GLANCE

—mber—

CARY GRANT, ROSALIND RUSSELL in

HIS GIRL FRIDAY Ⓐ

— Also —

...LE in JIGGS AND MAGGIE IN SOCIETY Ⓑ

—ember—

..RDON JACKSON, RONA ANDERSON in

FLOODTIDE Ⓐ

— Also —

SCOTT BRADY in CANON CITY Ⓐ

—ember—

..CHARD BASEHART, SCOTT BRADY in

HE WALKED BY NIGHT Ⓐ

— Also —

..RR, ROBERT CUMMINGS in LET'S LIVE A LITTLE Ⓐ

—ptember—

..AN SIMMONS, DONALD HOUSTON in

Monday, 19th September—

NORMAN WOOLAND, SARAH CH..

ALL OVER THE TO..

— Also —

FREDRIC MARCH, DAN DUR..

ANOTHER PART OF THE ..

Thursday, 22nd September—

BOB HOPE, LUCILLE BAL..

SORROWFUL JON..

Monday, 26th September—

BURT LANCASTER, JOAN FON..

BLOOD ON MY HA..

— Also —

ROD CAMERON, MARIA MON..

PIRATES OF MONTERE..

Thursday, 29th September—

LINDA DARNELL, ANN SOTH..

3

5

Printed in Great Britain
by Amazon

32626409R00119